SPROCKET

Volume 2

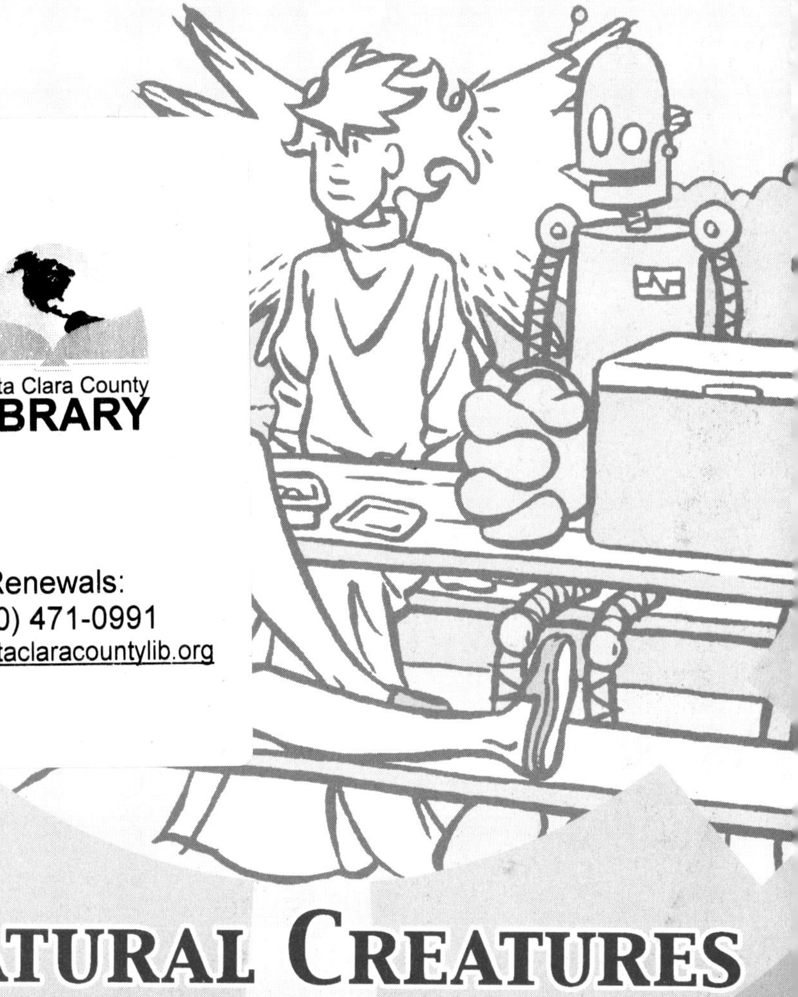

NATURAL CREATURES

by Kerry Callen

A series by Kerry Callen angelrobot@hotmail
www.haloandsprocket.com

To Ellen, Anna, Chris, Martin, and
scattered friends –
Rich

Mike

Anna Maria

Nate

Keith

Halo and Sprocket (Volume 2): Natural Creatures

"Same Difference", "Face It", "Tune Out", and "Watch This" originally published in the
Kansas City Star, November 4, 11, 18, and 25, 2004. "Head Games" originally appeared in
the *STAPLE!, the Independent Media Expo* program book, 2008. All other material
previously unpublished.

Published by Amaze Ink, a division of SLG Publishing, P.O. Box 26427, San Jose,
CA 95159-6427.

Dan Vado – President & Publisher
Jennifer de Guzman – Editor-in-Chief

www.slgcomic.com.

First Edition: July 2008

PRINTED IN CANADA

ISBN: 978-159362-131-5

HALO AND SPROCKET

"DISTURBING MATTERS"

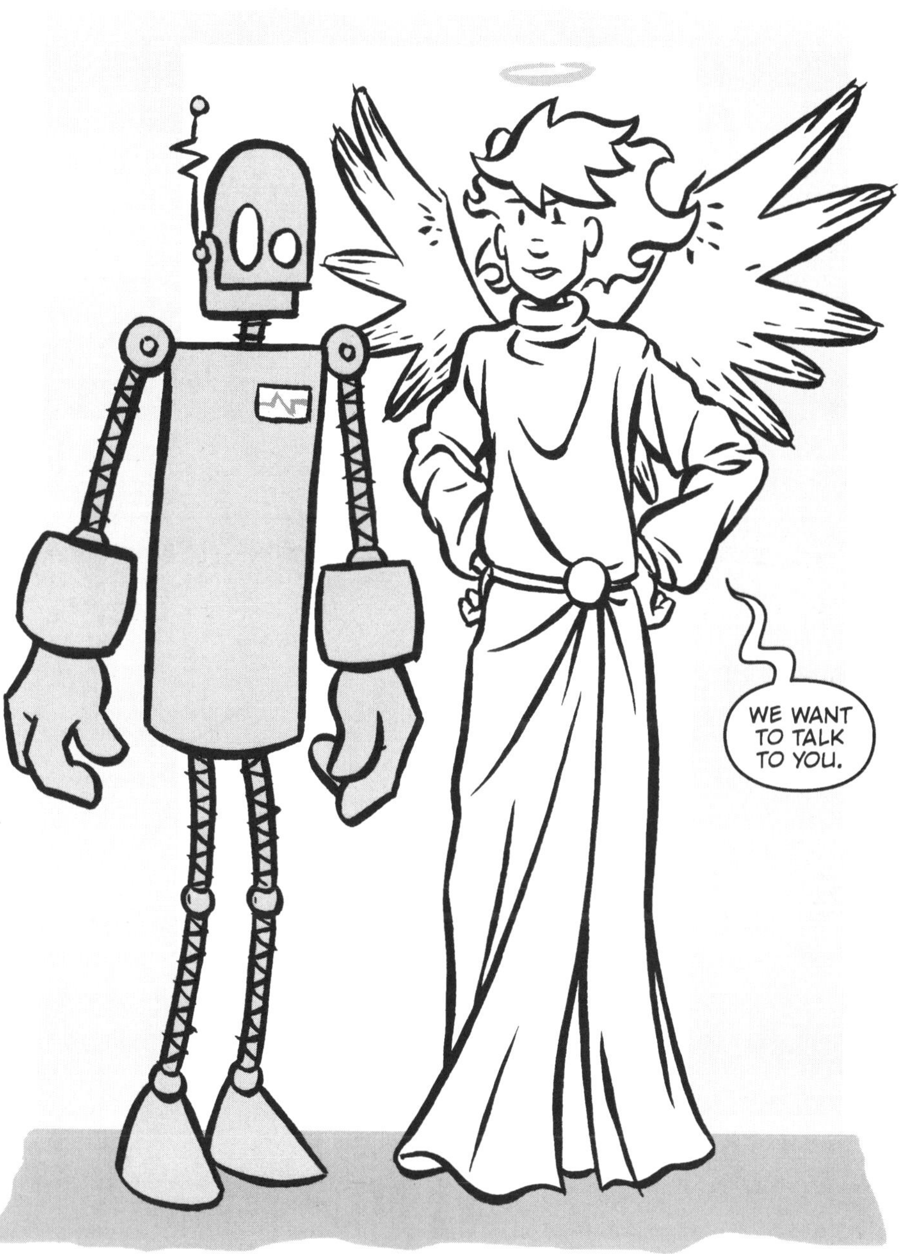
WE WANT TO TALK TO YOU.

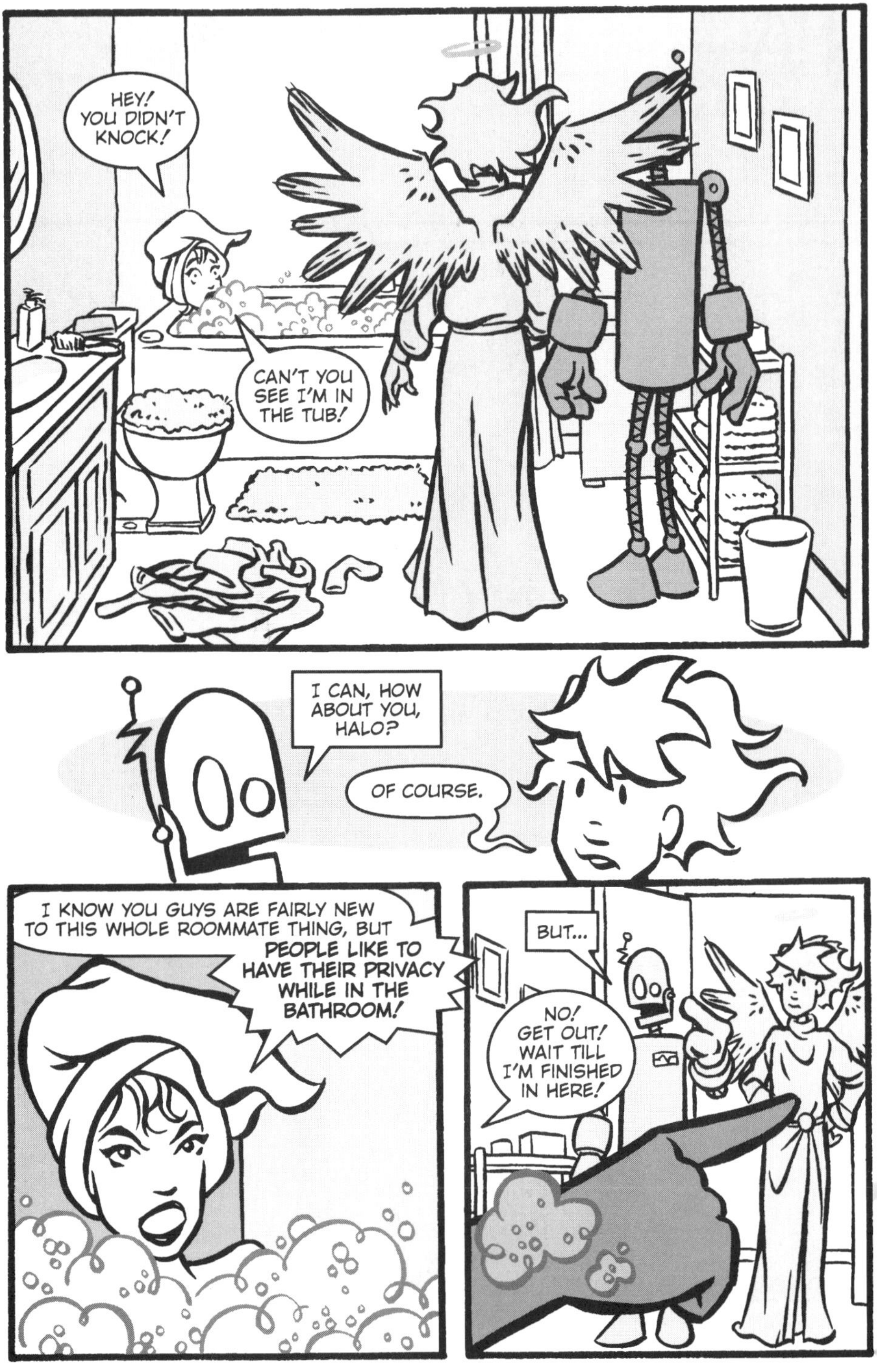
HEY! YOU DIDN'T KNOCK!
CAN'T YOU SEE I'M IN THE TUB!
I CAN, HOW ABOUT YOU, HALO?
OF COURSE.
I KNOW YOU GUYS ARE FAIRLY NEW TO THIS WHOLE ROOMMATE THING, BUT PEOPLE LIKE TO HAVE THEIR PRIVACY WHILE IN THE BATHROOM!
BUT...
NO! GET OUT! WAIT TILL I'M FINISHED IN HERE!

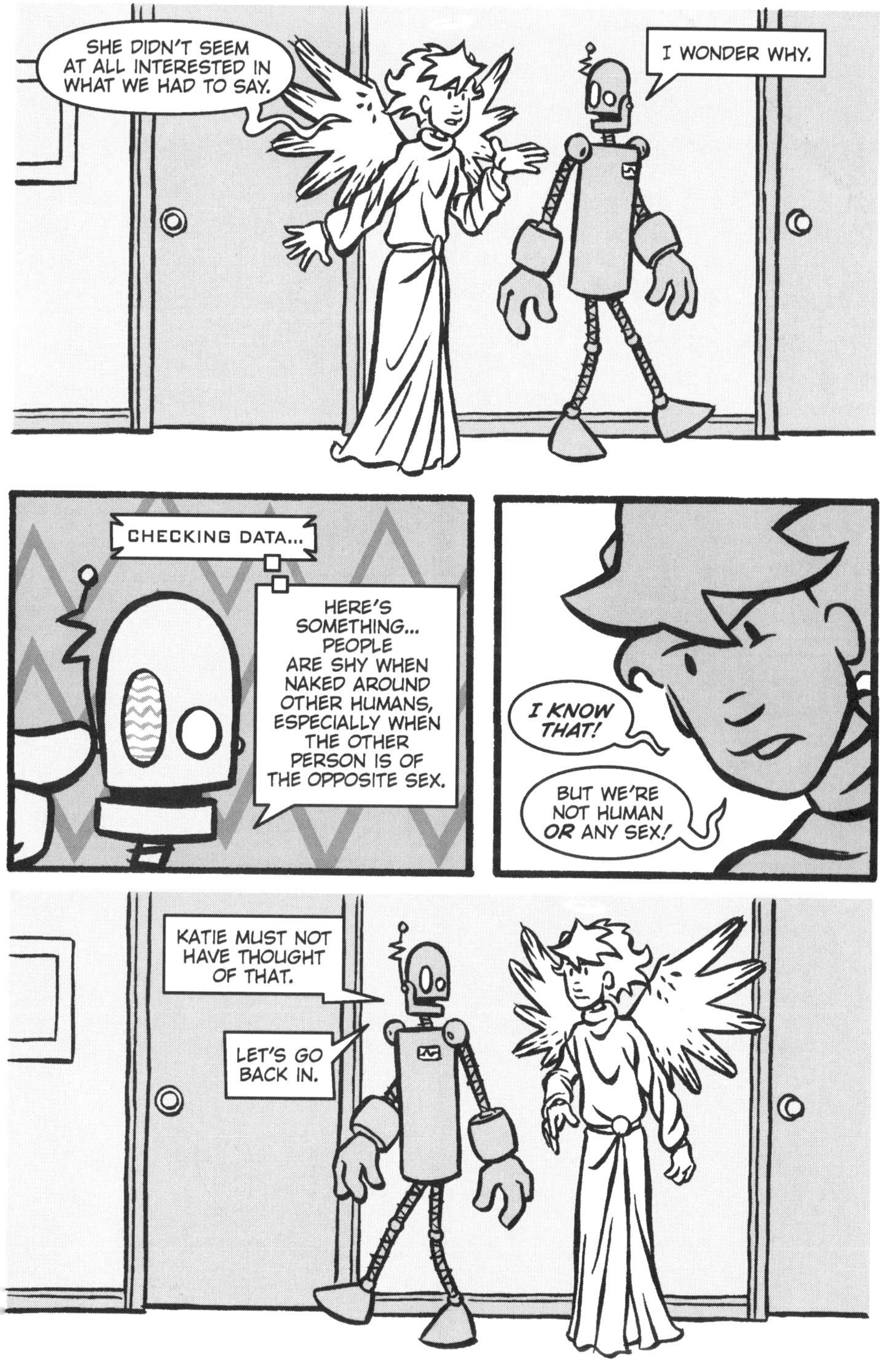
SHE DIDN'T SEEM AT ALL INTERESTED IN WHAT WE HAD TO SAY.
I WONDER WHY.
CHECKING DATA...
HERE'S SOMETHING... PEOPLE ARE SHY WHEN NAKED AROUND OTHER HUMANS, ESPECIALLY WHEN THE OTHER PERSON IS OF THE OPPOSITE SEX.
I KNOW THAT!
BUT WE'RE NOT HUMAN OR ANY SEX!
KATIE MUST NOT HAVE THOUGHT OF THAT.
LET'S GO BACK IN.

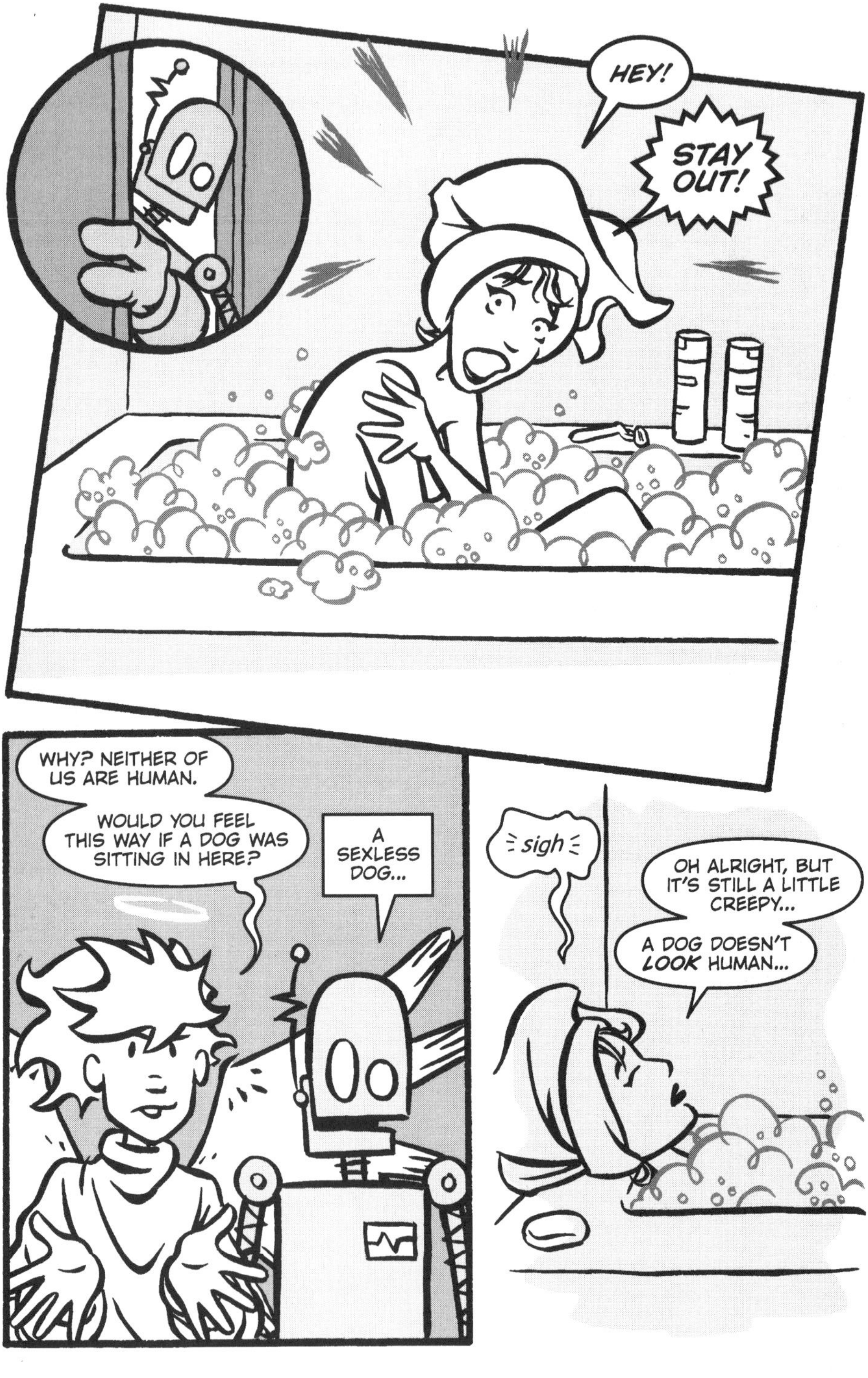
HEY!
STAY OUT!
WHY? NEITHER OF US ARE HUMAN.
WOULD YOU FEEL THIS WAY IF A DOG WAS SITTING IN HERE?
A SEXLESS DOG...
sigh
OH ALRIGHT, BUT IT'S STILL A LITTLE CREEPY...
A DOG DOESN'T *LOOK* HUMAN...

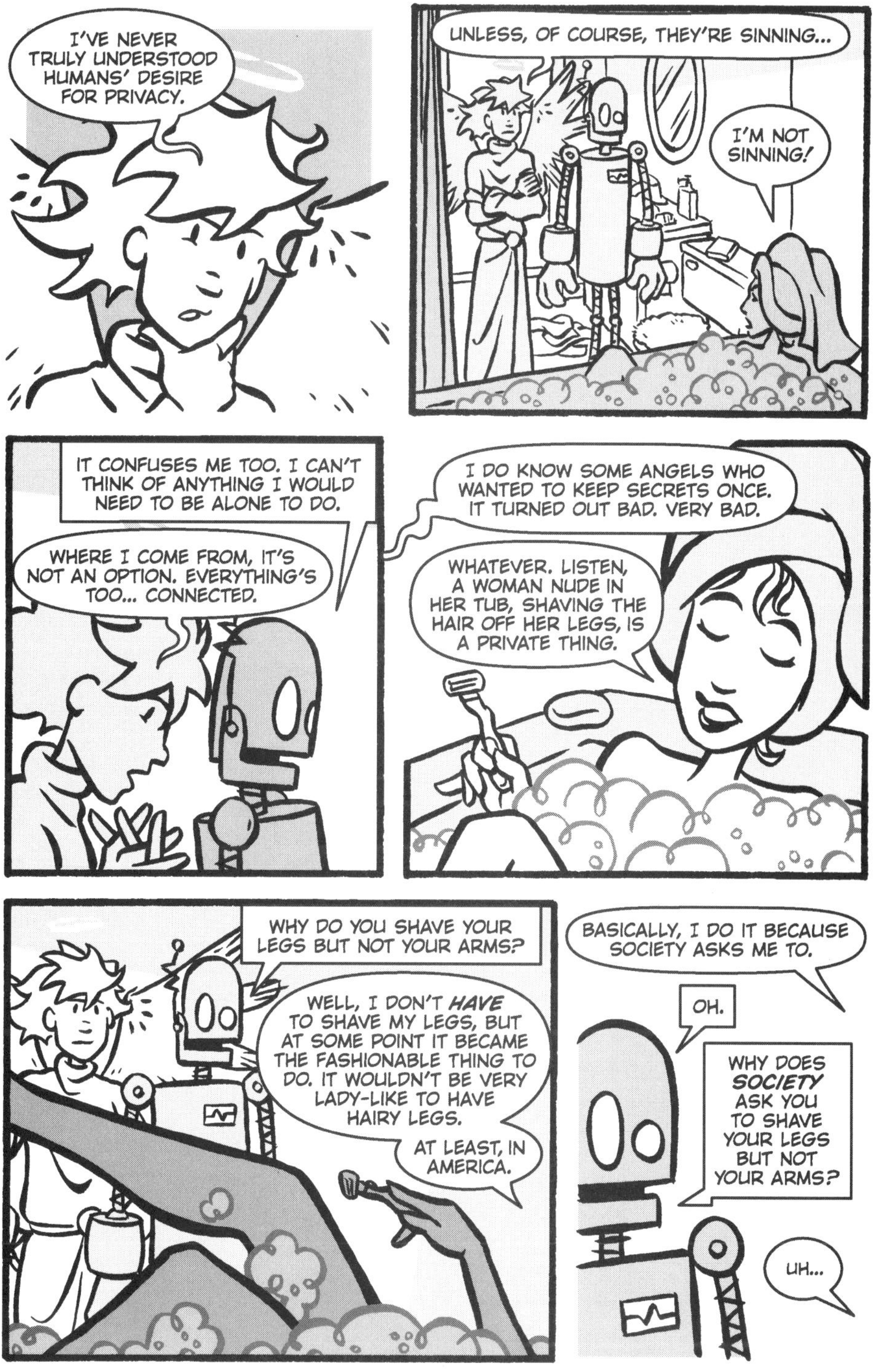
I'VE NEVER TRULY UNDERSTOOD HUMANS' DESIRE FOR PRIVACY.
UNLESS, OF COURSE, THEY'RE SINNING...
I'M NOT SINNING!
IT CONFUSES ME TOO. I CAN'T THINK OF ANYTHING I WOULD NEED TO BE ALONE TO DO.
WHERE I COME FROM, IT'S NOT AN OPTION. EVERYTHING'S TOO... CONNECTED.
I DO KNOW SOME ANGELS WHO WANTED TO KEEP SECRETS ONCE. IT TURNED OUT BAD. VERY BAD.
WHATEVER. LISTEN, A WOMAN NUDE IN HER TUB, SHAVING THE HAIR OFF HER LEGS, IS A PRIVATE THING.
WHY DO YOU SHAVE YOUR LEGS BUT NOT YOUR ARMS?
WELL, I DON'T *HAVE* TO SHAVE MY LEGS, BUT AT SOME POINT IT BECAME THE FASHIONABLE THING TO DO. IT WOULDN'T BE VERY LADY-LIKE TO HAVE HAIRY LEGS.
AT LEAST, IN AMERICA.
BASICALLY, I DO IT BECAUSE SOCIETY ASKS ME TO.
OH.
WHY DOES *SOCIETY* ASK YOU TO SHAVE YOUR LEGS BUT NOT YOUR ARMS?
UH...

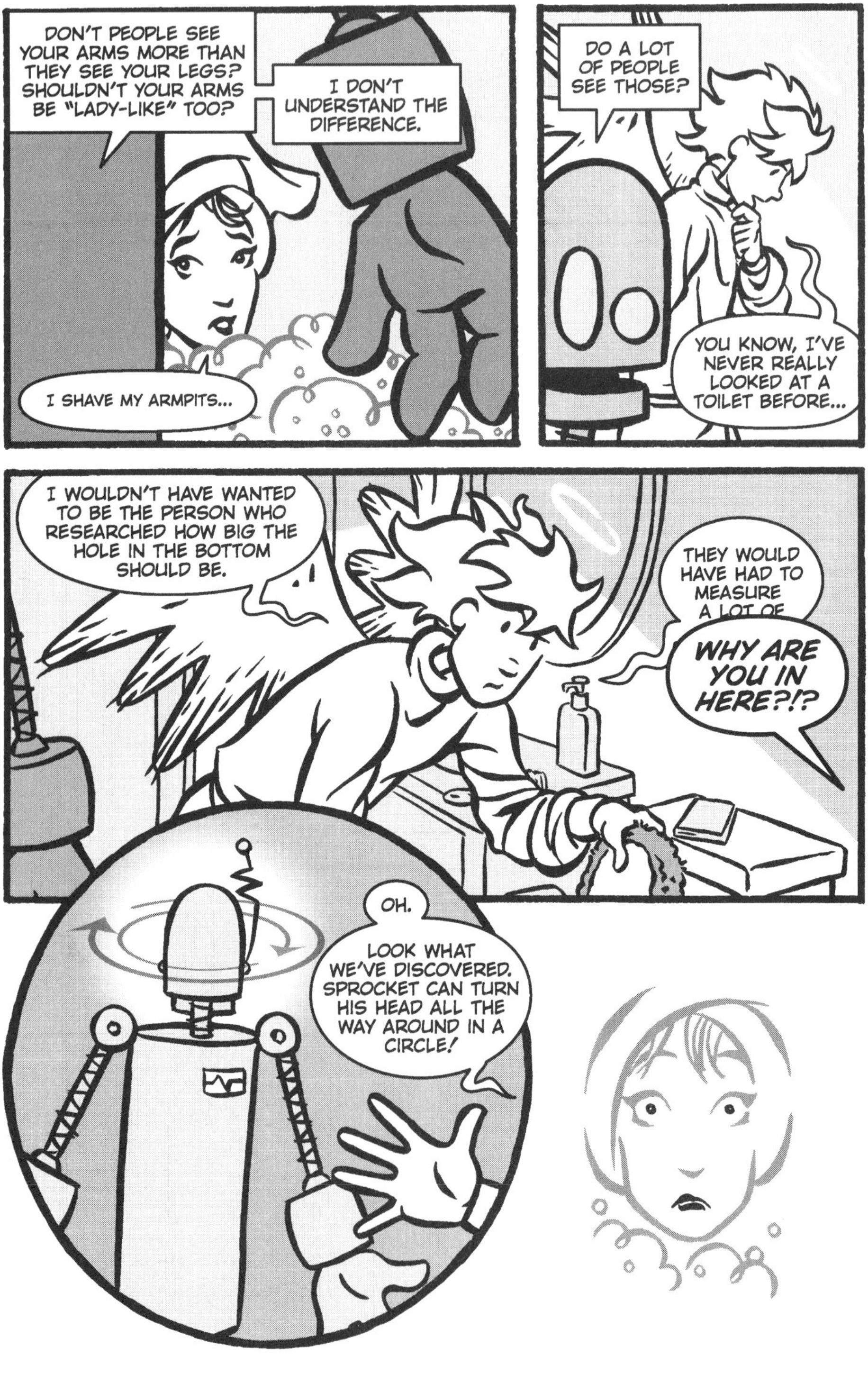
DON'T PEOPLE SEE YOUR ARMS MORE THAN THEY SEE YOUR LEGS? SHOULDN'T YOUR ARMS BE "LADY-LIKE" TOO?
I DON'T UNDERSTAND THE DIFFERENCE.
I SHAVE MY ARMPITS...
DO A LOT OF PEOPLE SEE THOSE?
YOU KNOW, I'VE NEVER REALLY LOOKED AT A TOILET BEFORE...
I WOULDN'T HAVE WANTED TO BE THE PERSON WHO RESEARCHED HOW BIG THE HOLE IN THE BOTTOM SHOULD BE.
THEY WOULD HAVE HAD TO MEASURE A LOT OF
WHY ARE YOU IN HERE?!?
OH.
LOOK WHAT WE'VE DISCOVERED. SPROCKET CAN TURN HIS HEAD ALL THE WAY AROUND IN A CIRCLE!

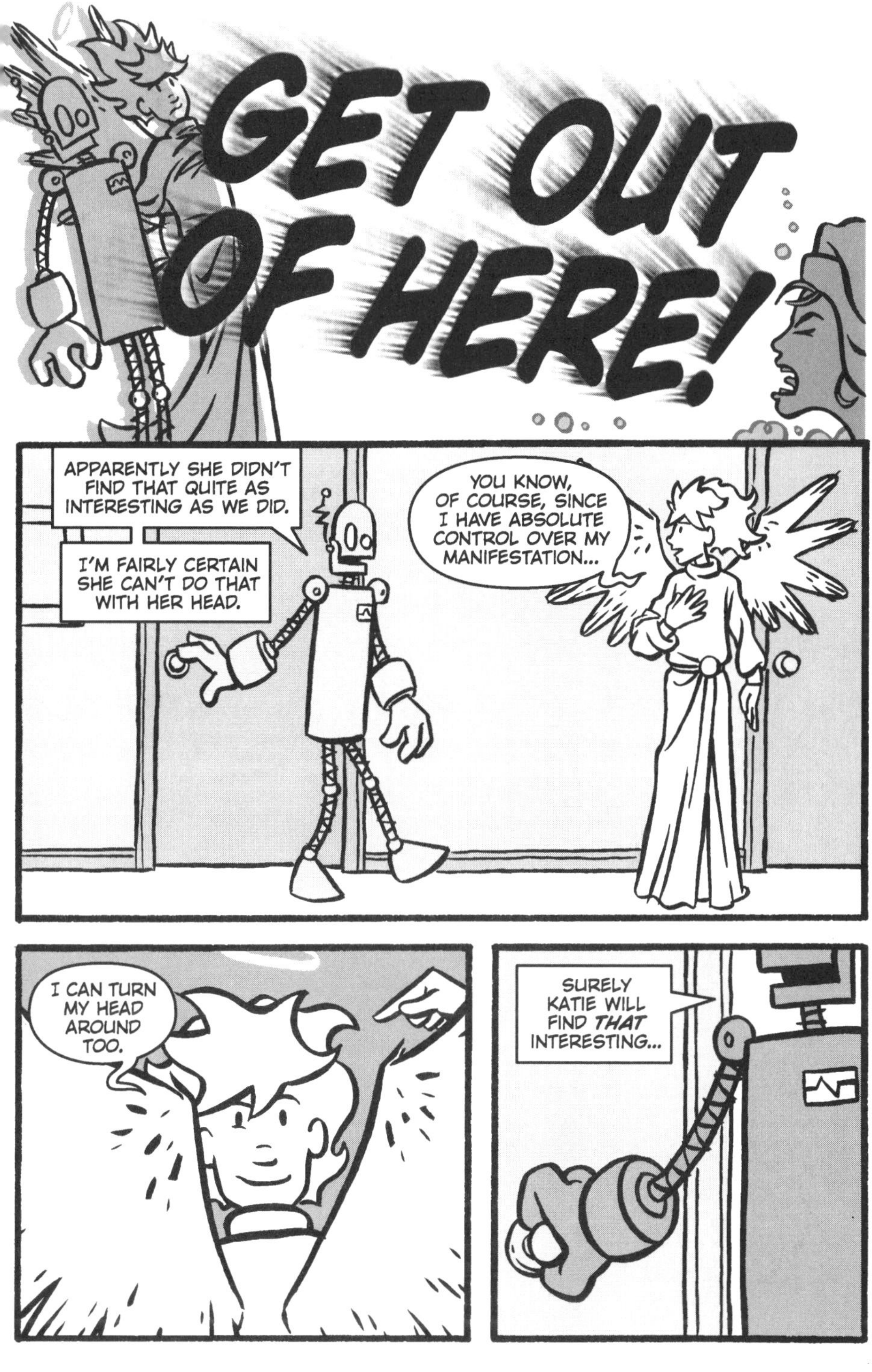
GET OUT OF HERE!
APPARENTLY SHE DIDN'T FIND THAT QUITE AS INTERESTING AS WE DID.
I'M FAIRLY CERTAIN SHE CAN'T DO THAT WITH HER HEAD.
YOU KNOW, OF COURSE, SINCE I HAVE ABSOLUTE CONTROL OVER MY MANIFESTATION...
I CAN TURN MY HEAD AROUND TOO.
SURELY KATIE WILL FIND *THAT* INTERESTING...

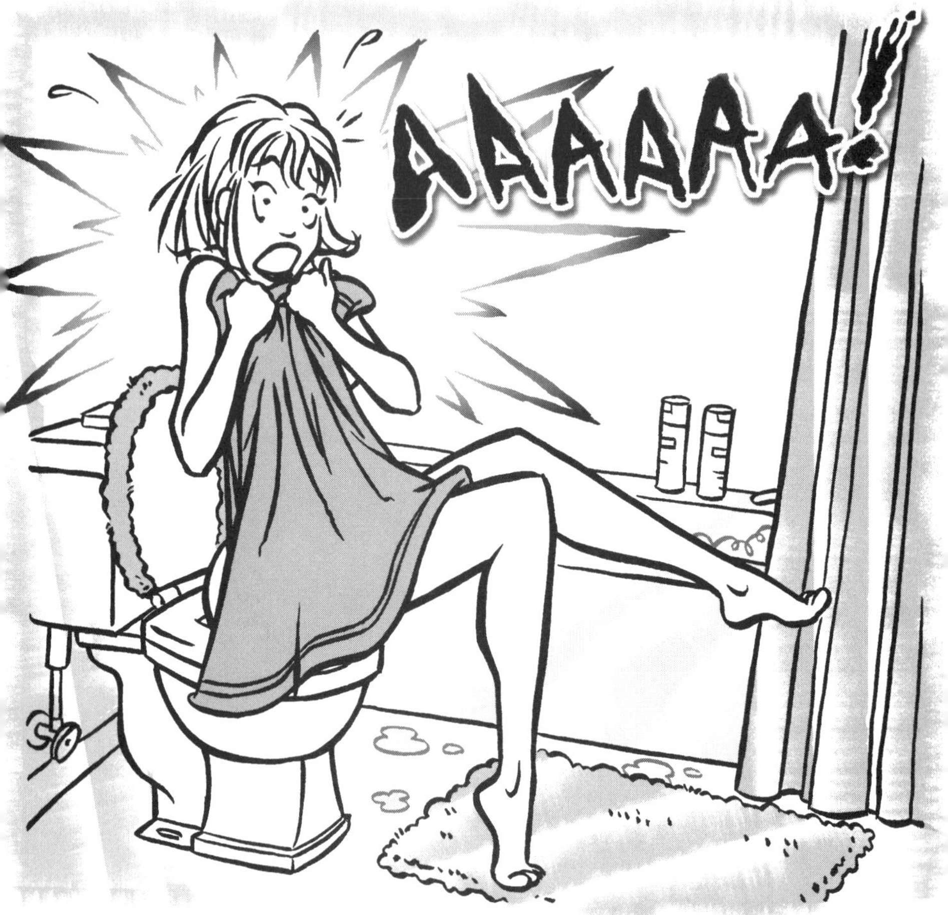
AAAAAA!

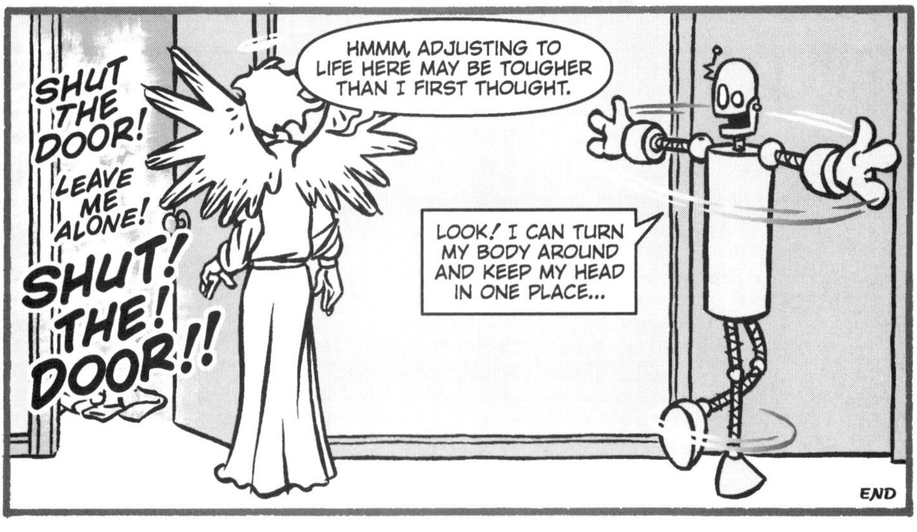
SHUT THE DOOR!
LEAVE ME ALONE!
SHUT! THE! DOOR!!
HMMM, ADJUSTING TO LIFE HERE MAY BE TOUGHER THAN I FIRST THOUGHT.
LOOK! I CAN TURN MY BODY AROUND AND KEEP MY HEAD IN ONE PLACE...
END

HALO AND SPROCKET

"NO BIG DEAL"

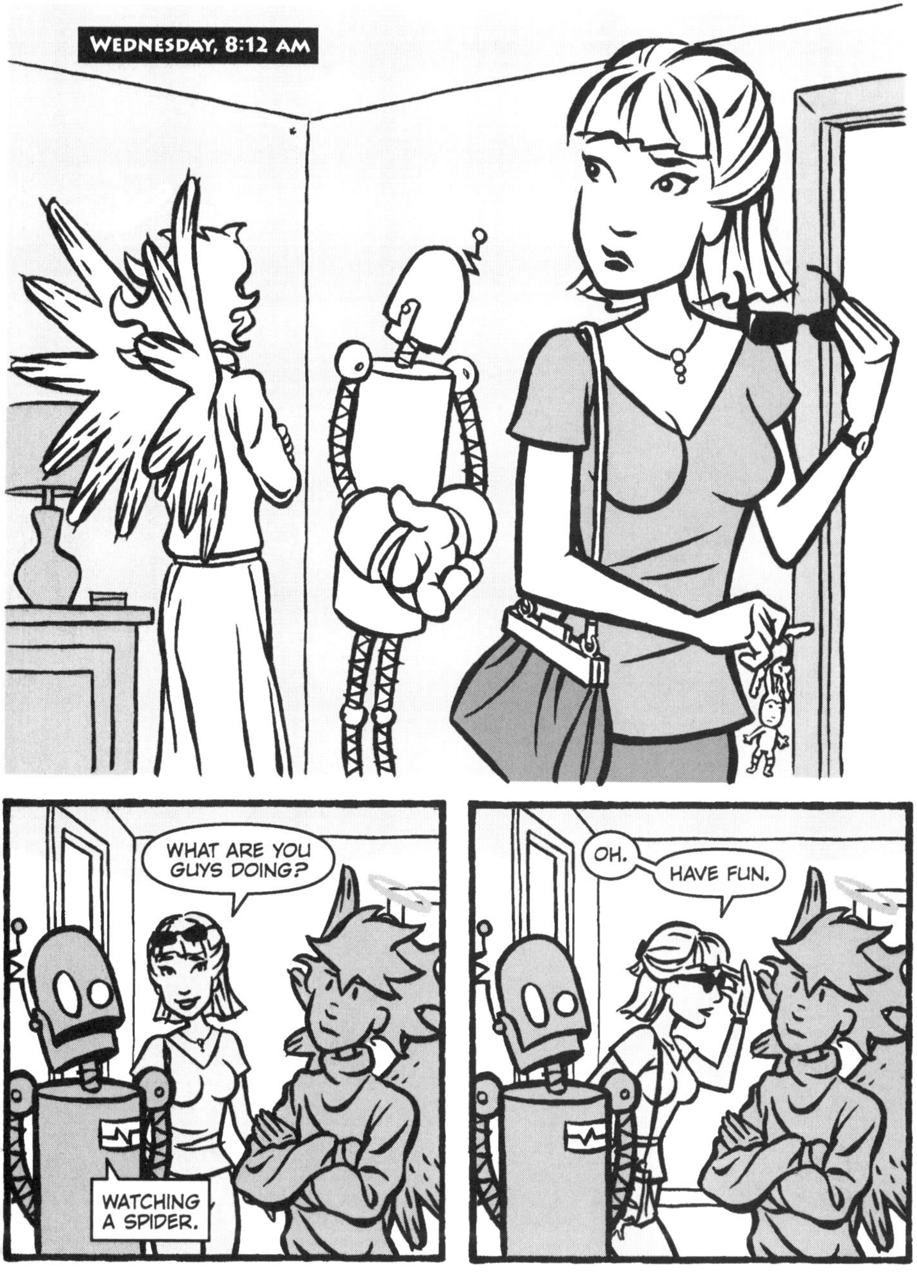

WEDNESDAY, 8:12 AM
WHAT ARE YOU GUYS DOING?
WATCHING A SPIDER.
OH.
HAVE FUN.

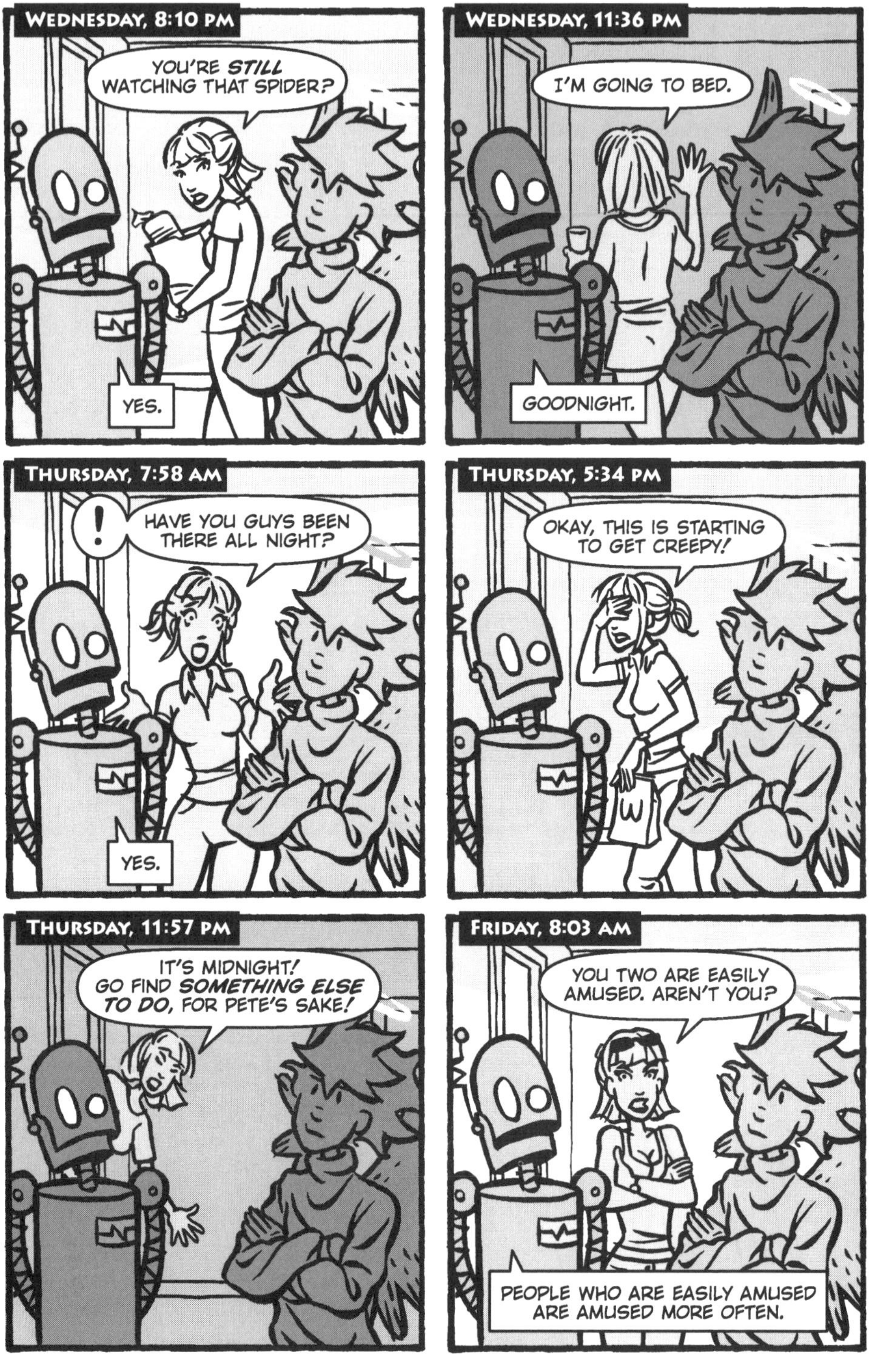
WEDNESDAY, 8:10 PM
YOU'RE STILL WATCHING THAT SPIDER?
YES.
WEDNESDAY, 11:36 PM
I'M GOING TO BED.
GOODNIGHT.
THURSDAY, 7:58 AM
!
HAVE YOU GUYS BEEN THERE ALL NIGHT?
YES.
THURSDAY, 5:34 PM
OKAY, THIS IS STARTING TO GET CREEPY!
W
THURSDAY, 11:57 PM
IT'S MIDNIGHT! GO FIND SOMETHING ELSE TO DO, FOR PETE'S SAKE!
FRIDAY, 8:03 AM
YOU TWO ARE EASILY AMUSED. AREN'T YOU?
PEOPLE WHO ARE EASILY AMUSED ARE AMUSED MORE OFTEN.

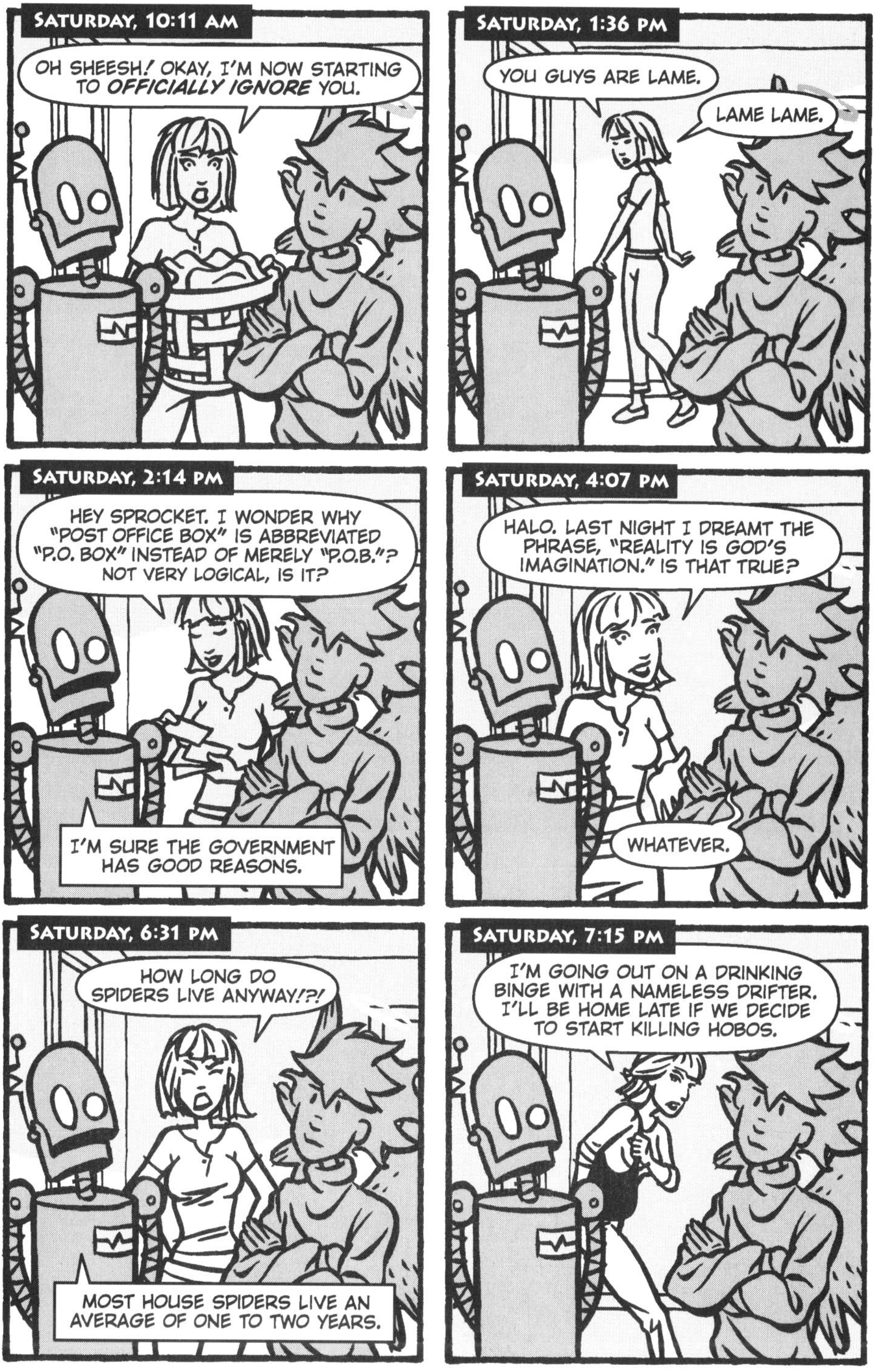
SATURDAY, 10:11 AM
OH SHEESH! OKAY, I'M NOW STARTING TO OFFICIALLY IGNORE YOU.
SATURDAY, 1:36 PM
YOU GUYS ARE LAME.
LAME LAME.
SATURDAY, 2:14 PM
HEY SPROCKET. I WONDER WHY "POST OFFICE BOX" IS ABBREVIATED "P.O. BOX" INSTEAD OF MERELY "P.O.B."? NOT VERY LOGICAL, IS IT?
I'M SURE THE GOVERNMENT HAS GOOD REASONS.
SATURDAY, 4:07 PM
HALO. LAST NIGHT I DREAMT THE PHRASE, "REALITY IS GOD'S IMAGINATION." IS THAT TRUE?
WHATEVER.
SATURDAY, 6:31 PM
HOW LONG DO SPIDERS LIVE ANYWAY!?!
MOST HOUSE SPIDERS LIVE AN AVERAGE OF ONE TO TWO YEARS.
SATURDAY, 7:15 PM
I'M GOING OUT ON A DRINKING BINGE WITH A NAMELESS DRIFTER. I'LL BE HOME LATE IF WE DECIDE TO START KILLING HOBOS.

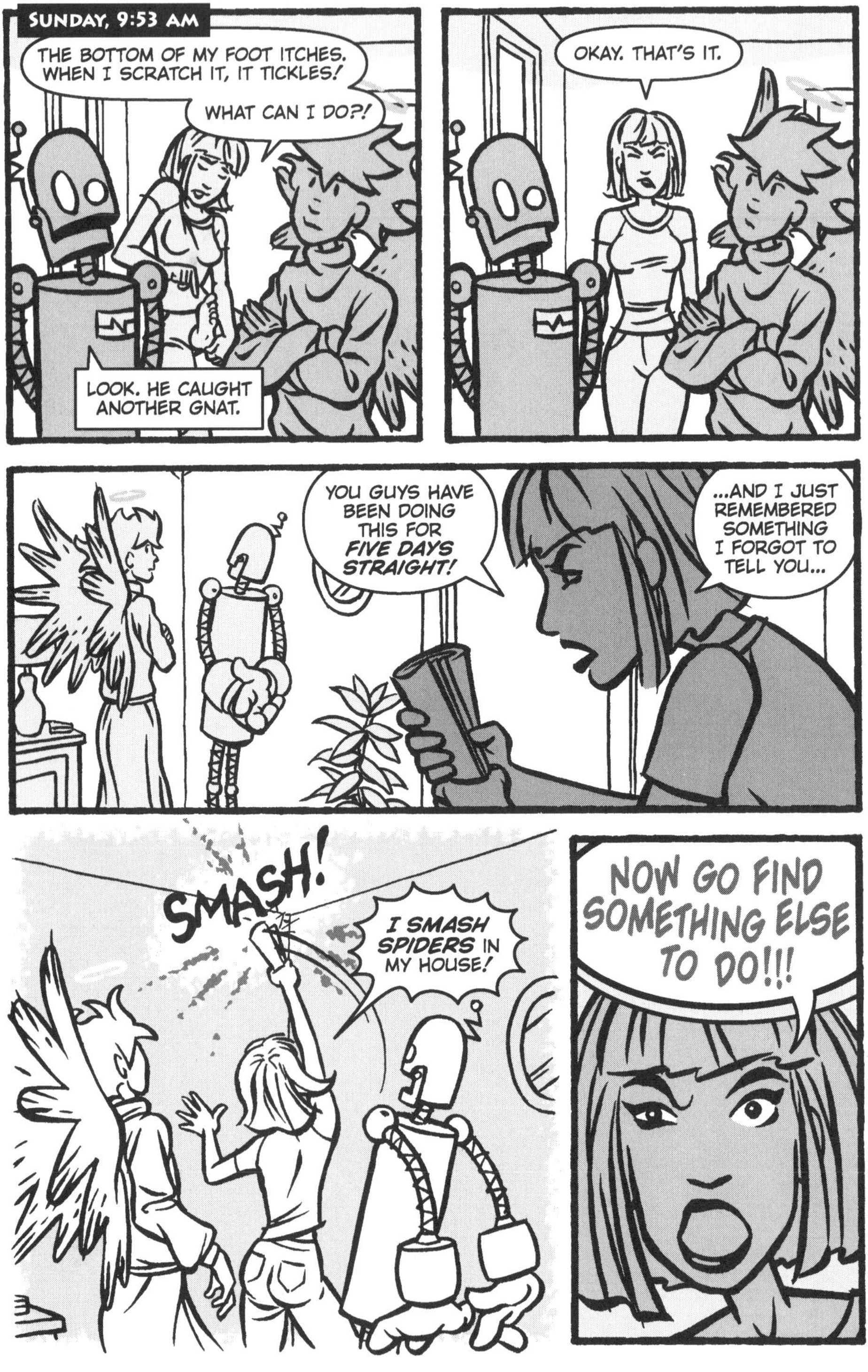
SUNDAY, 9:53 AM
THE BOTTOM OF MY FOOT ITCHES. WHEN I SCRATCH IT, IT TICKLES!
WHAT CAN I DO?!
LOOK. HE CAUGHT ANOTHER GNAT.
OKAY. THAT'S IT.
YOU GUYS HAVE BEEN DOING THIS FOR *FIVE DAYS STRAIGHT!*
...AND I JUST REMEMBERED SOMETHING I FORGOT TO TELL YOU...
SMASH!
I SMASH SPIDERS IN MY HOUSE!
NOW GO FIND SOMETHING ELSE TO DO!!!

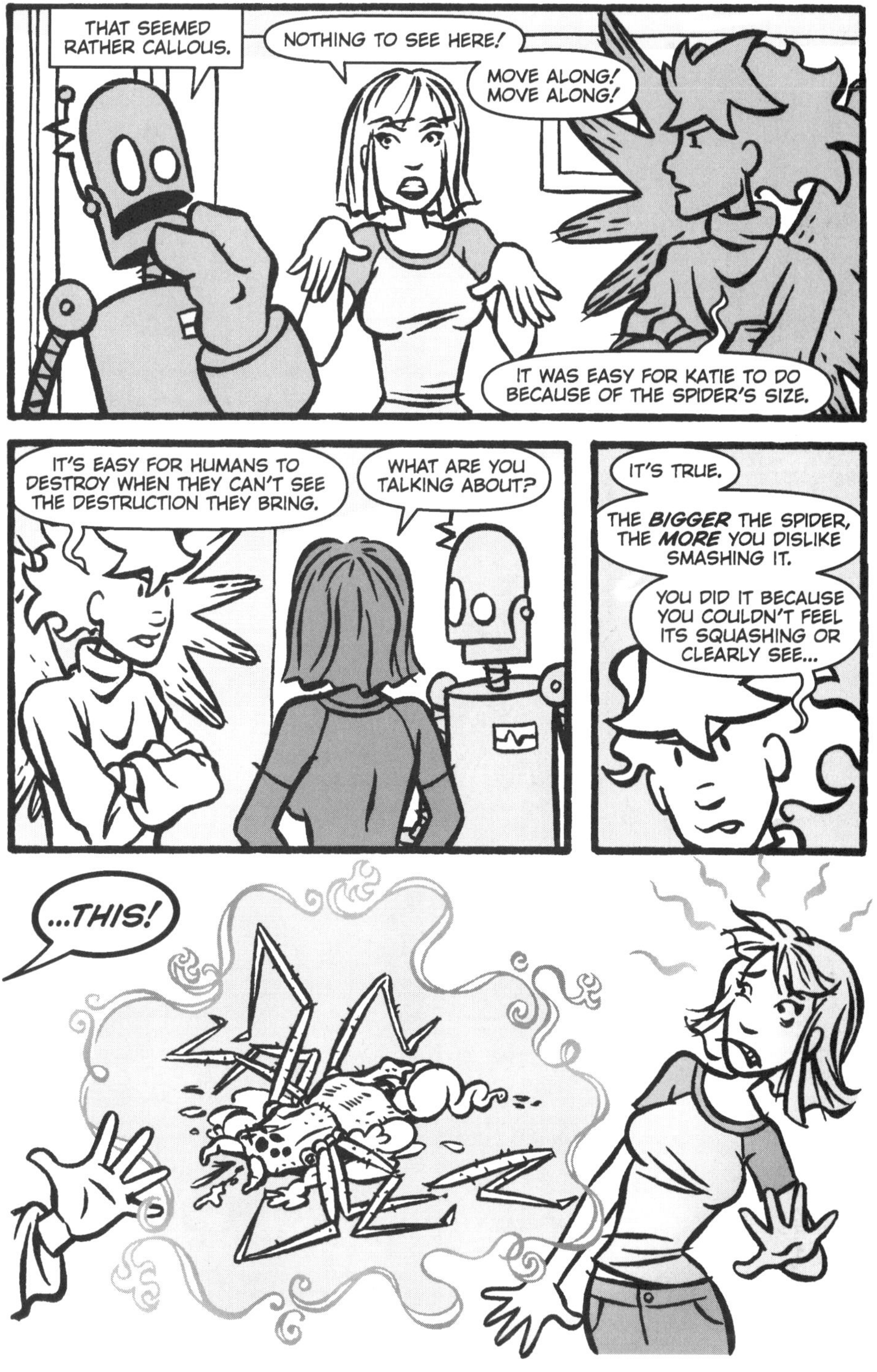
THAT SEEMED RATHER CALLOUS.
NOTHING TO SEE HERE!
MOVE ALONG! MOVE ALONG!
IT WAS EASY FOR KATIE TO DO BECAUSE OF THE SPIDER'S SIZE.
IT'S EASY FOR HUMANS TO DESTROY WHEN THEY CAN'T SEE THE DESTRUCTION THEY BRING.
WHAT ARE YOU TALKING ABOUT?
IT'S TRUE.
THE *BIGGER* THE SPIDER, THE *MORE* YOU DISLIKE SMASHING IT.
YOU DID IT BECAUSE YOU COULDN'T FEEL ITS SQUASHING OR CLEARLY SEE...
...THIS!

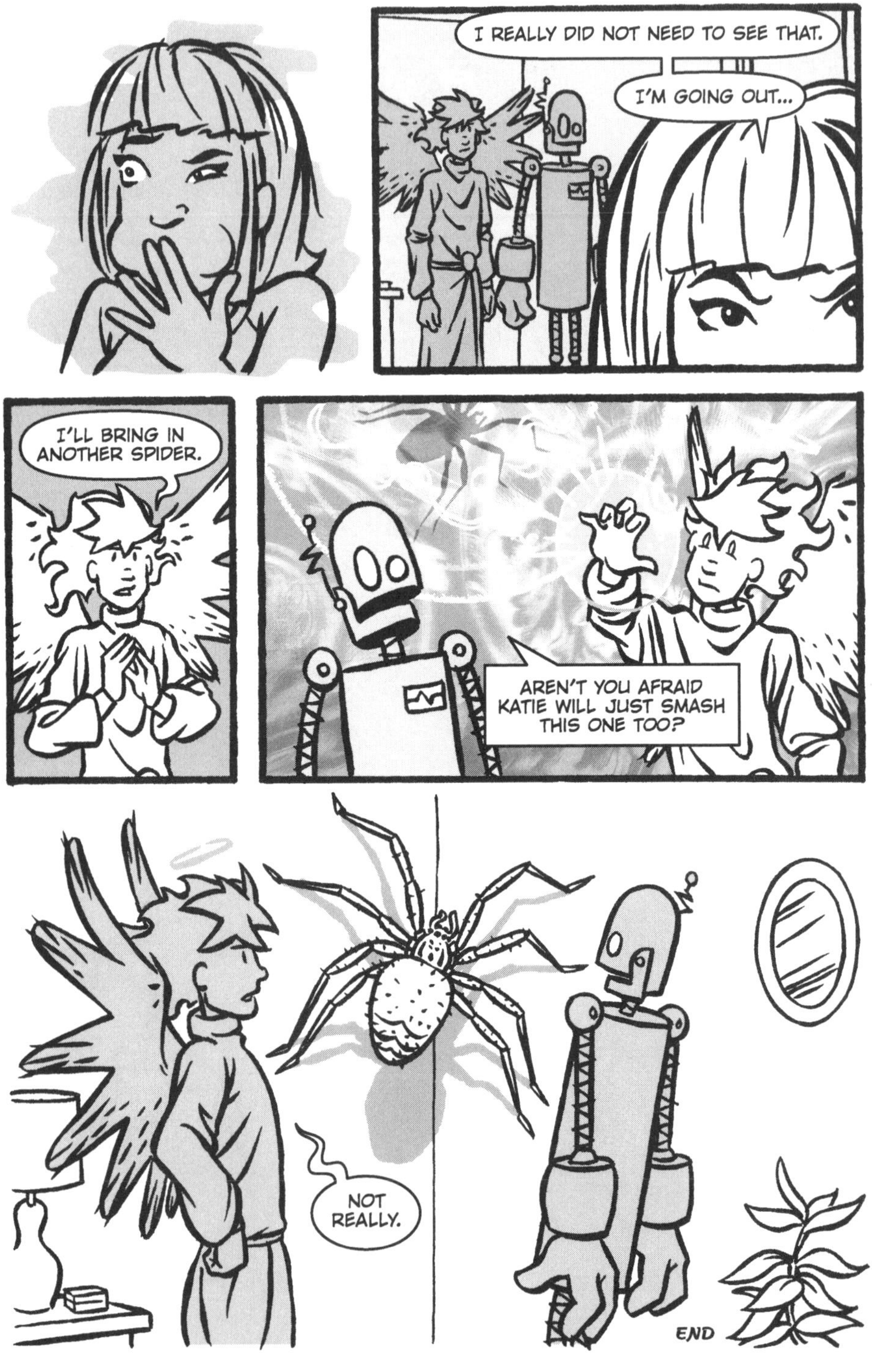

I REALLY DID NOT NEED TO SEE THAT.
I'M GOING OUT...
I'LL BRING IN ANOTHER SPIDER.
AREN'T YOU AFRAID KATIE WILL JUST SMASH THIS ONE TOO?
NOT REALLY.
END

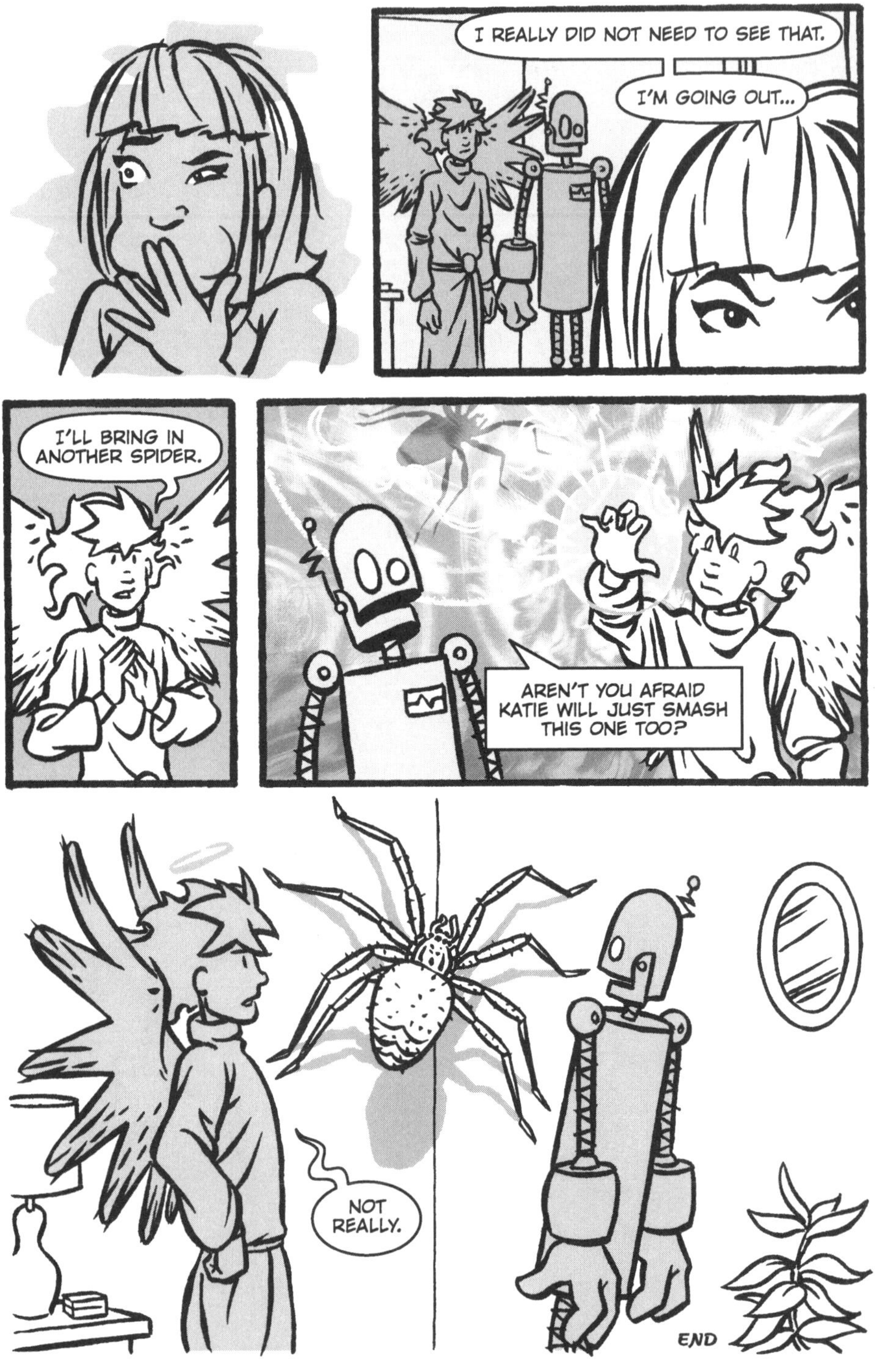
I REALLY DID NOT NEED TO SEE THAT.
I'M GOING OUT...
I'LL BRING IN ANOTHER SPIDER.
AREN'T YOU AFRAID KATIE WILL JUST SMASH THIS ONE TOO?
NOT REALLY.
END

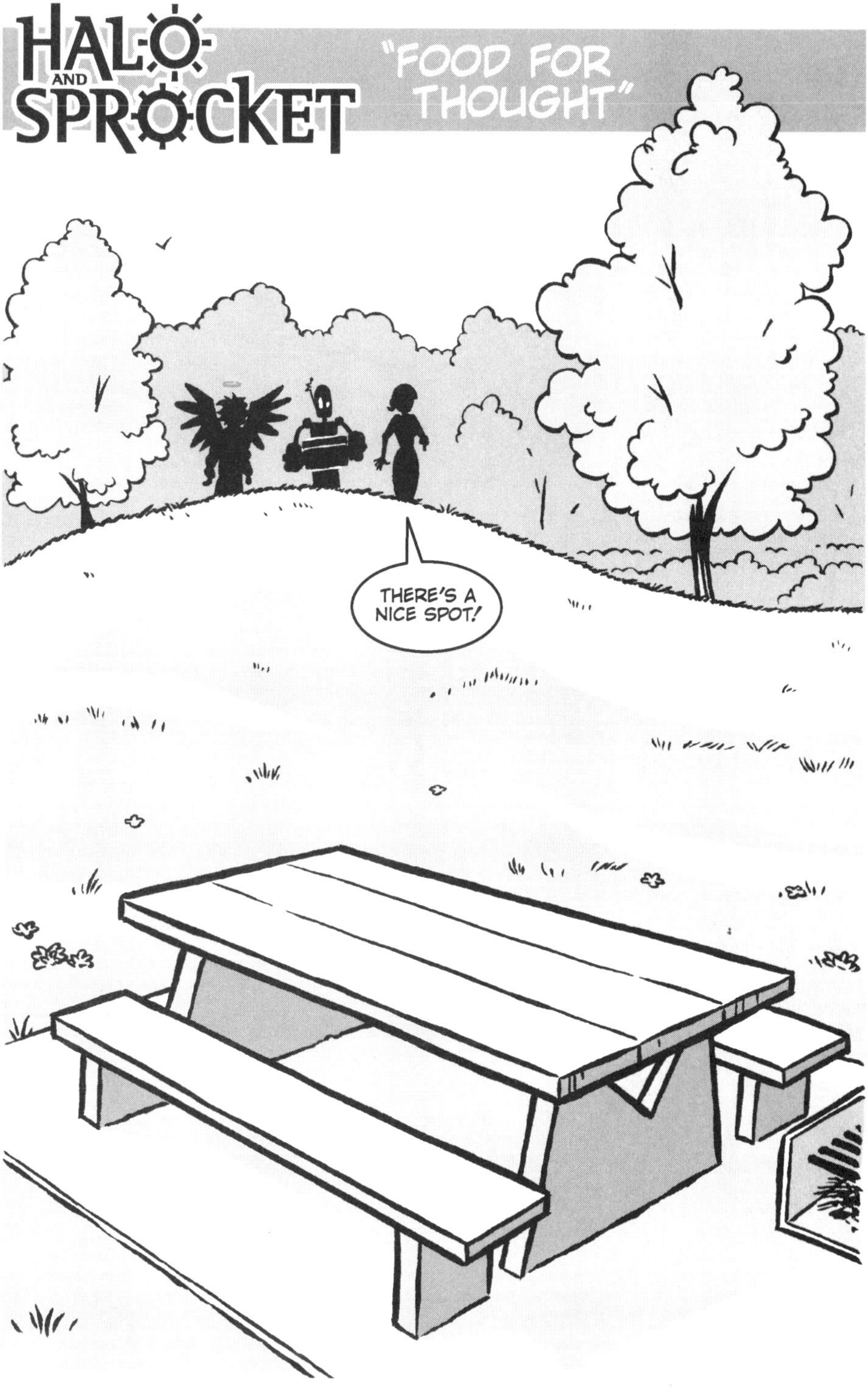
HALO AND SPROCKET
"FOOD FOR THOUGHT"
THERE'S A NICE SPOT!

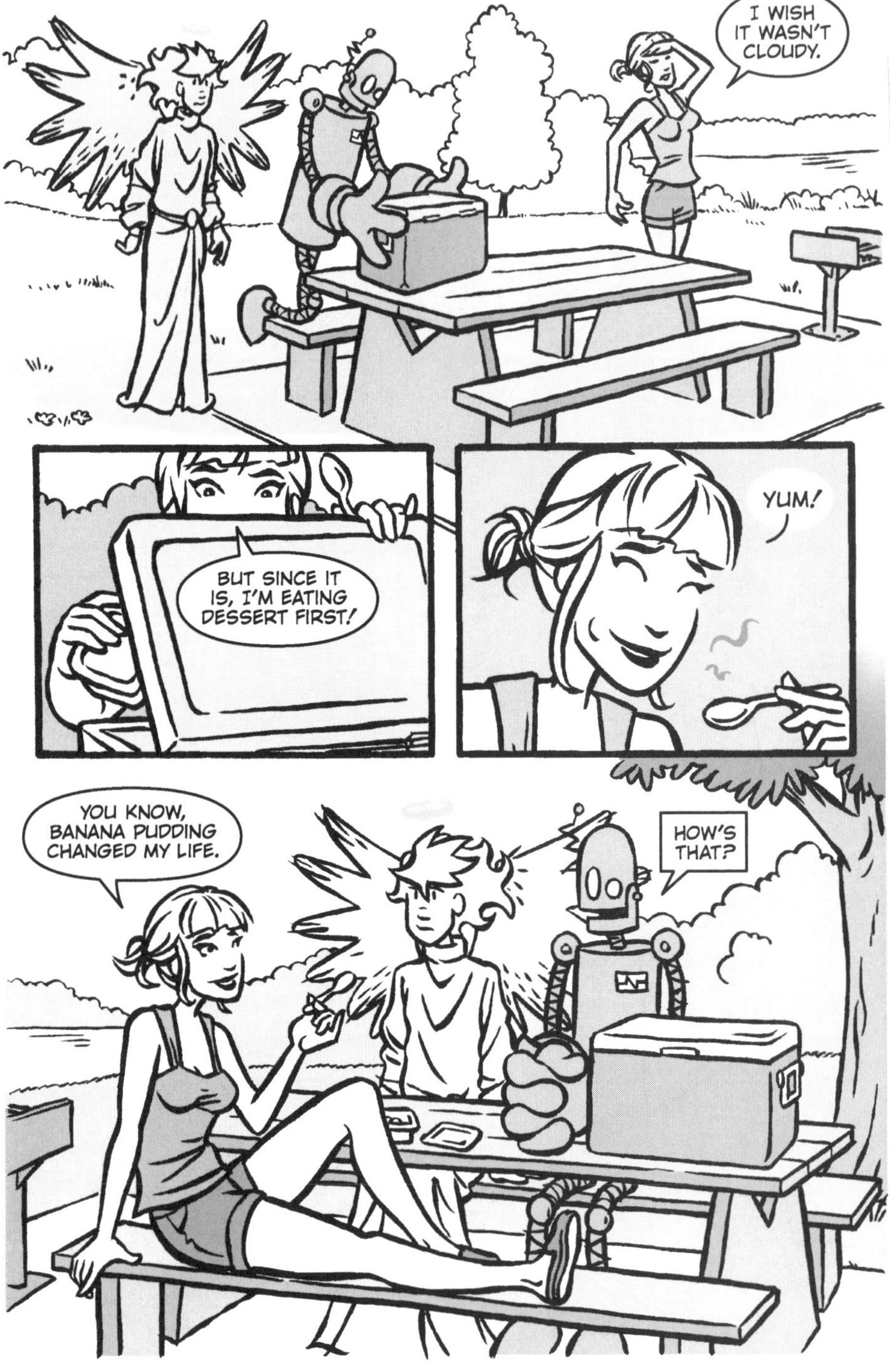
I WISH IT WASN'T CLOUDY.
BUT SINCE IT IS, I'M EATING DESSERT FIRST!
YUM!
YOU KNOW, BANANA PUDDING CHANGED MY LIFE.
HOW'S THAT?

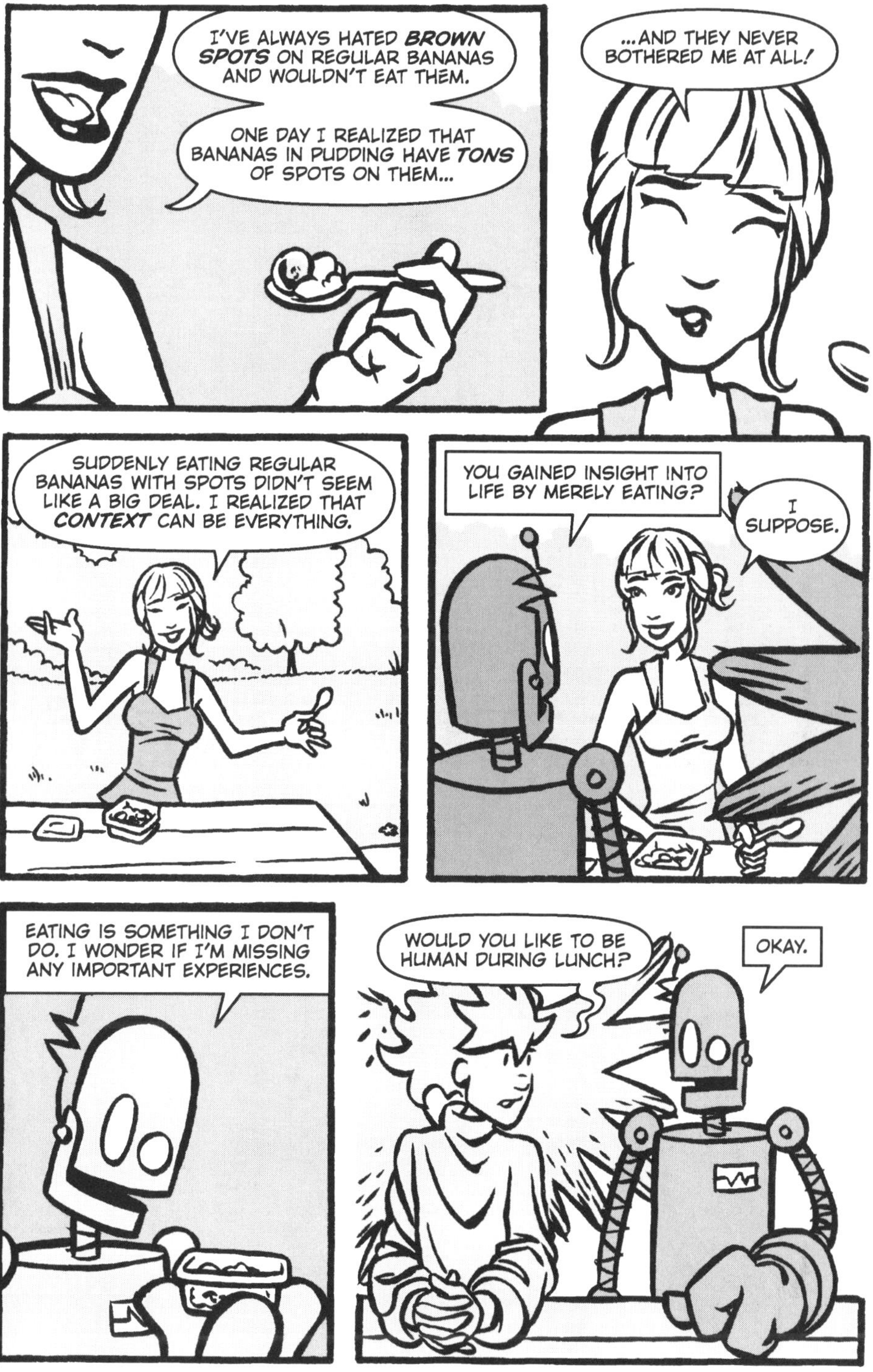
I'VE ALWAYS HATED BROWN SPOTS ON REGULAR BANANAS AND WOULDN'T EAT THEM.
ONE DAY I REALIZED THAT BANANAS IN PUDDING HAVE TONS OF SPOTS ON THEM...
...AND THEY NEVER BOTHERED ME AT ALL!
SUDDENLY EATING REGULAR BANANAS WITH SPOTS DIDN'T SEEM LIKE A BIG DEAL. I REALIZED THAT CONTEXT CAN BE EVERYTHING.
YOU GAINED INSIGHT INTO LIFE BY MERELY EATING?
I SUPPOSE.
EATING IS SOMETHING I DON'T DO. I WONDER IF I'M MISSING ANY IMPORTANT EXPERIENCES.
WOULD YOU LIKE TO BE HUMAN DURING LUNCH?
OKAY.

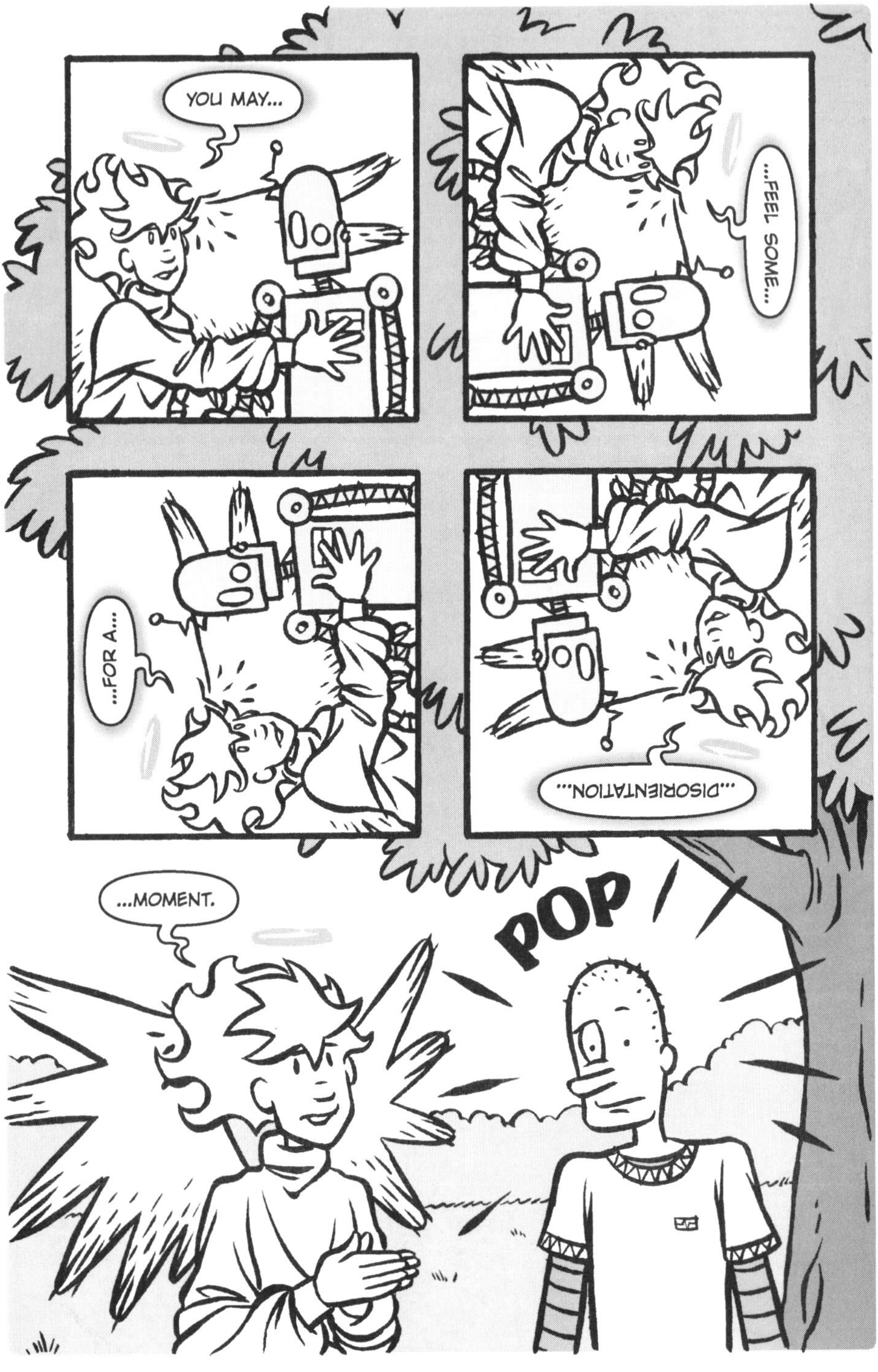
YOU MAY...
...FEEL SOME...
...FOR A...
...DISORIENTATION...
...MOMENT.
POP

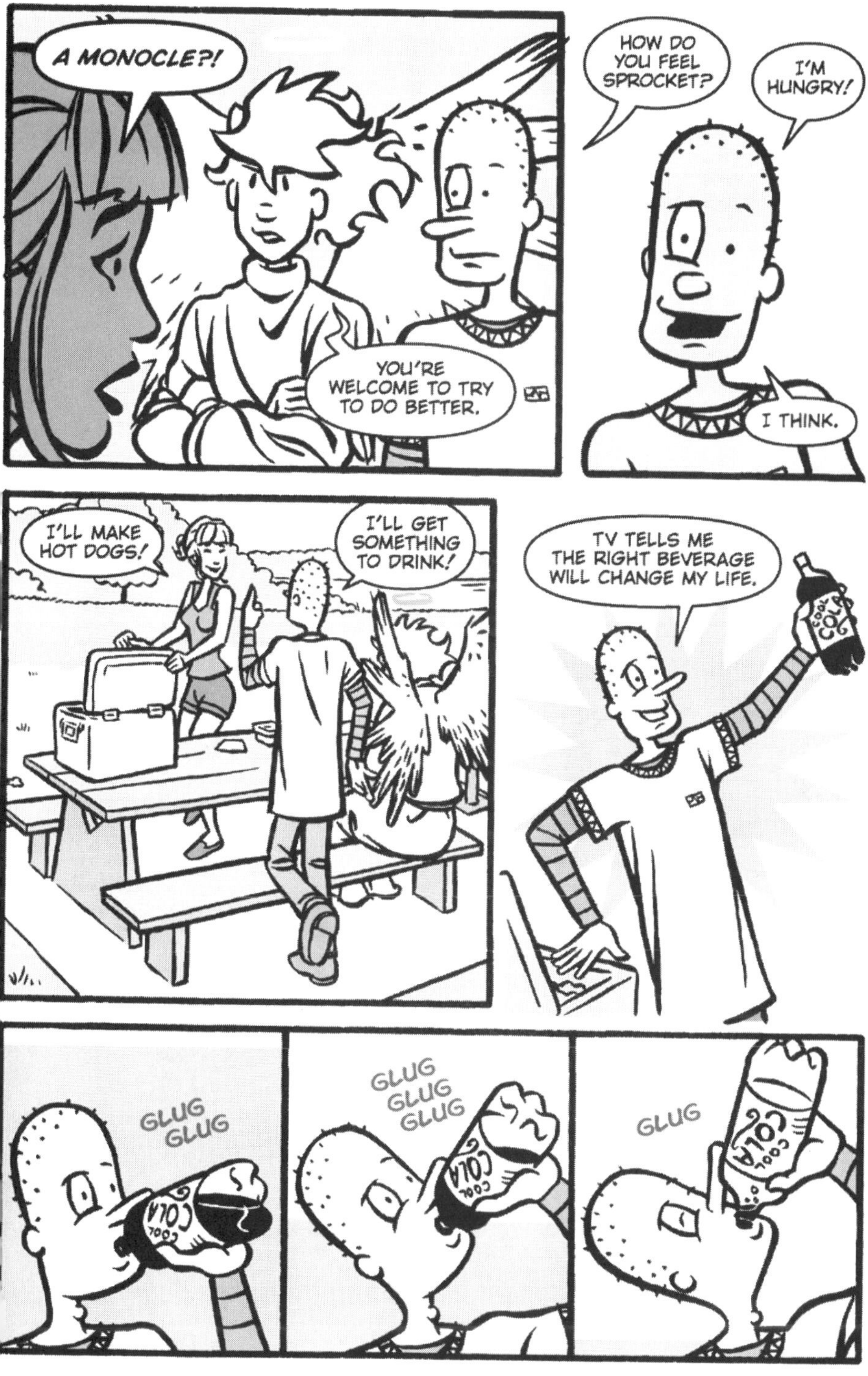
A MONOCLE?!
YOU'RE WELCOME TO TRY TO DO BETTER.
HOW DO YOU FEEL SPROCKET?
I'M HUNGRY!
I THINK.
I'LL MAKE HOT DOGS!
I'LL GET SOMETHING TO DRINK!
TV TELLS ME THE RIGHT BEVERAGE WILL CHANGE MY LIFE.
COOL COLA
GLUG GLUG
COOL COLA
GLUG GLUG GLUG
COOL COLA
GLUG
COOL COLA

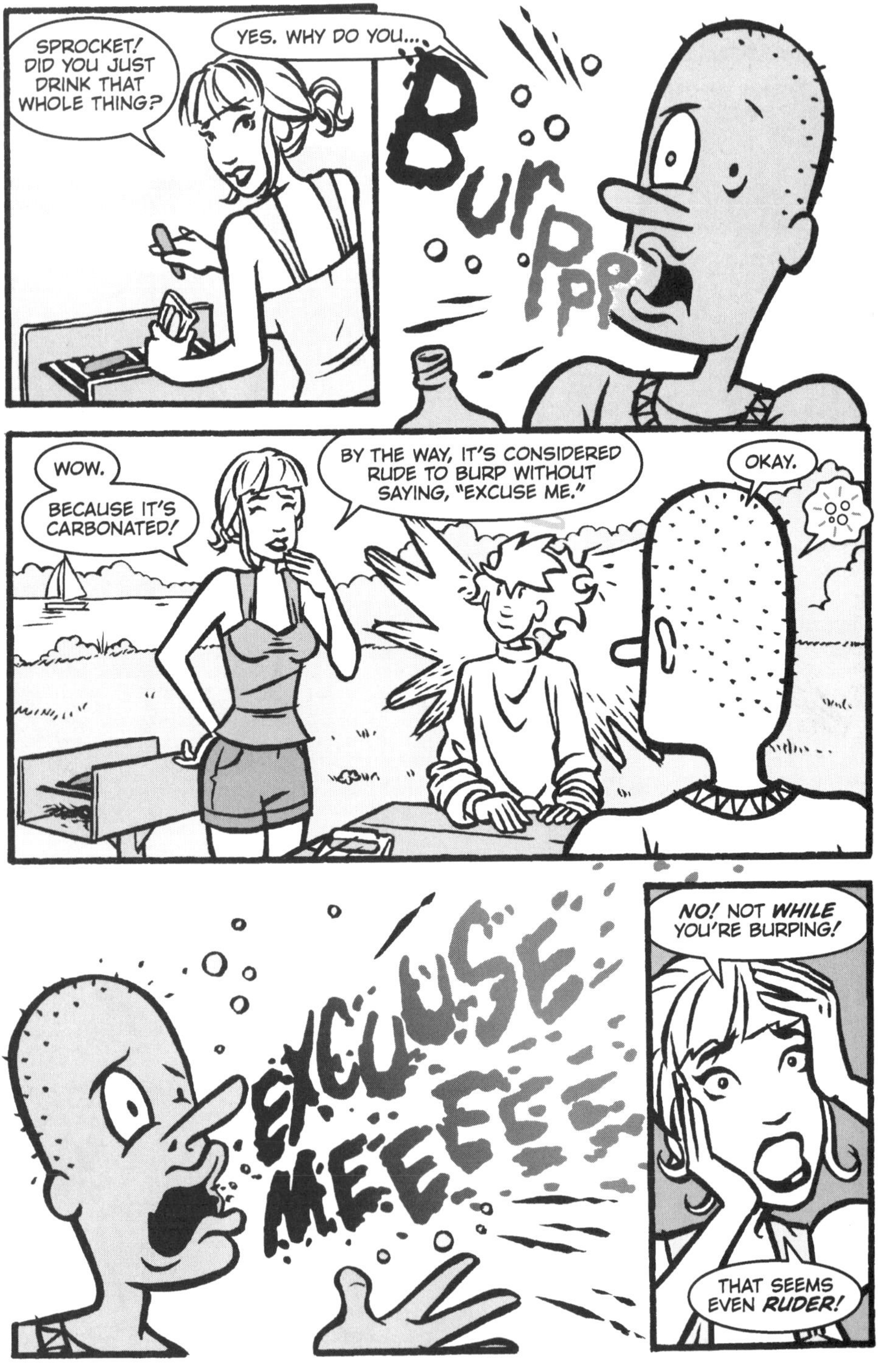
SPROCKET! DID YOU JUST DRINK THAT WHOLE THING?
YES. WHY DO YOU...
BURPPP
WOW.
BECAUSE IT'S CARBONATED!
BY THE WAY, IT'S CONSIDERED RUDE TO BURP WITHOUT SAYING, "EXCUSE ME."
OKAY.
EXCUUSE MEEEE
NO! NOT WHILE YOU'RE BURPING!
THAT SEEMS EVEN RUDER!

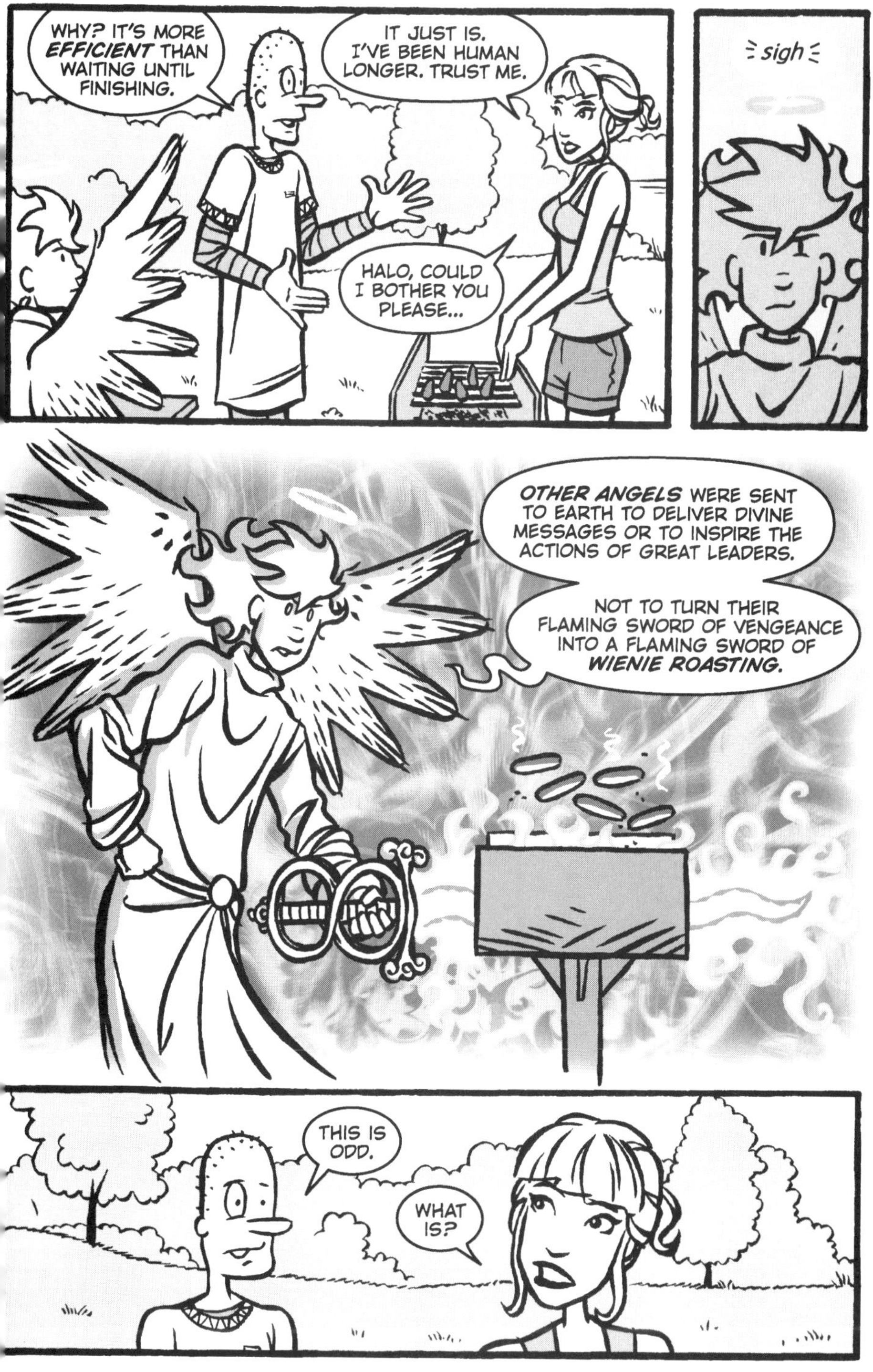
WHY? IT'S MORE EFFICIENT THAN WAITING UNTIL FINISHING.
IT JUST IS. I'VE BEEN HUMAN LONGER. TRUST ME.
HALO, COULD I BOTHER YOU PLEASE...
sigh
OTHER ANGELS WERE SENT TO EARTH TO DELIVER DIVINE MESSAGES OR TO INSPIRE THE ACTIONS OF GREAT LEADERS.
NOT TO TURN THEIR FLAMING SWORD OF VENGEANCE INTO A FLAMING SWORD OF WIENIE ROASTING.
THIS IS ODD.
WHAT IS?

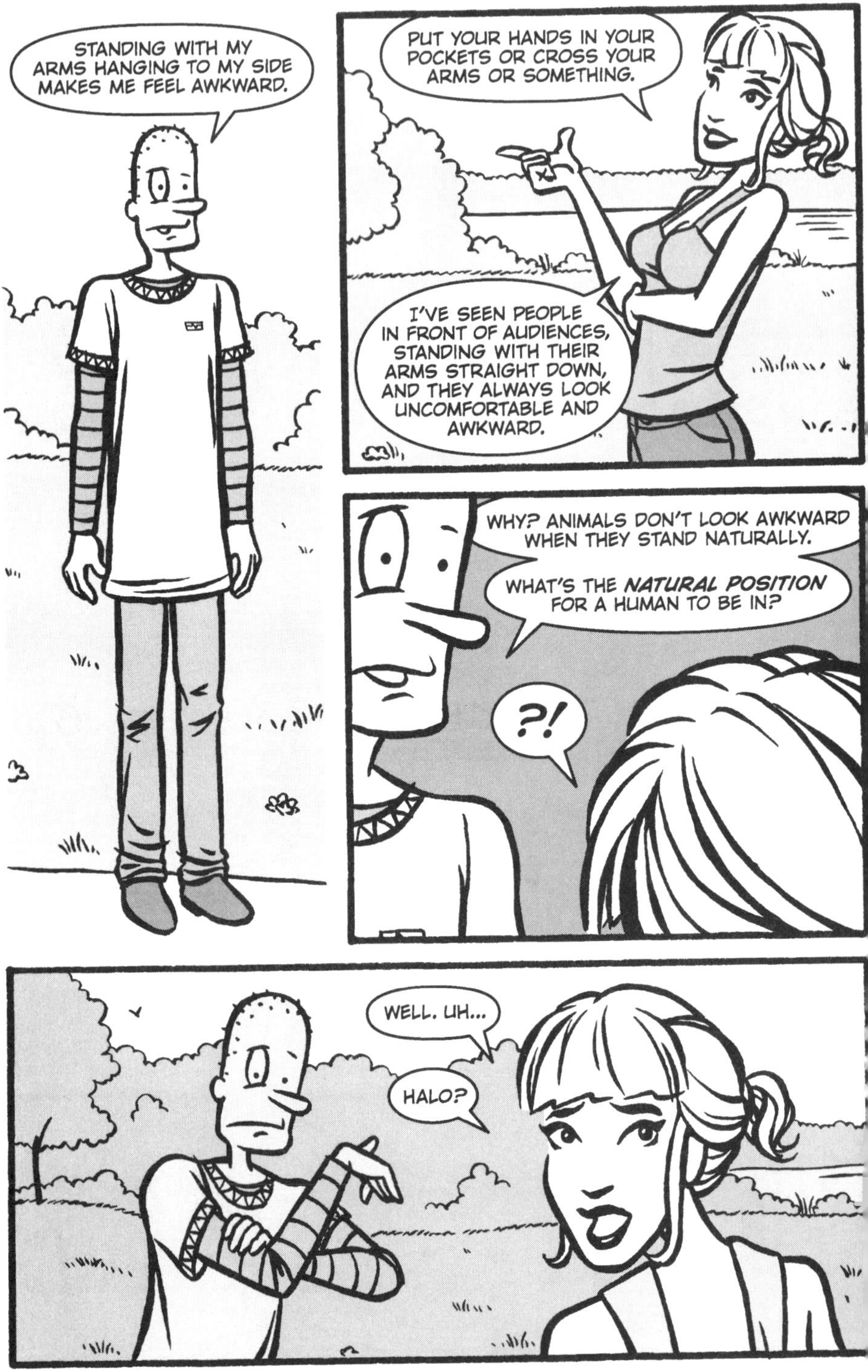
STANDING WITH MY ARMS HANGING TO MY SIDE MAKES ME FEEL AWKWARD.
PUT YOUR HANDS IN YOUR POCKETS OR CROSS YOUR ARMS OR SOMETHING.
I'VE SEEN PEOPLE IN FRONT OF AUDIENCES, STANDING WITH THEIR ARMS STRAIGHT DOWN, AND THEY ALWAYS LOOK UNCOMFORTABLE AND AWKWARD.
WHY? ANIMALS DON'T LOOK AWKWARD WHEN THEY STAND NATURALLY.
WHAT'S THE *NATURAL POSITION* FOR A HUMAN TO BE IN?
?!
WELL. UH...
HALO?

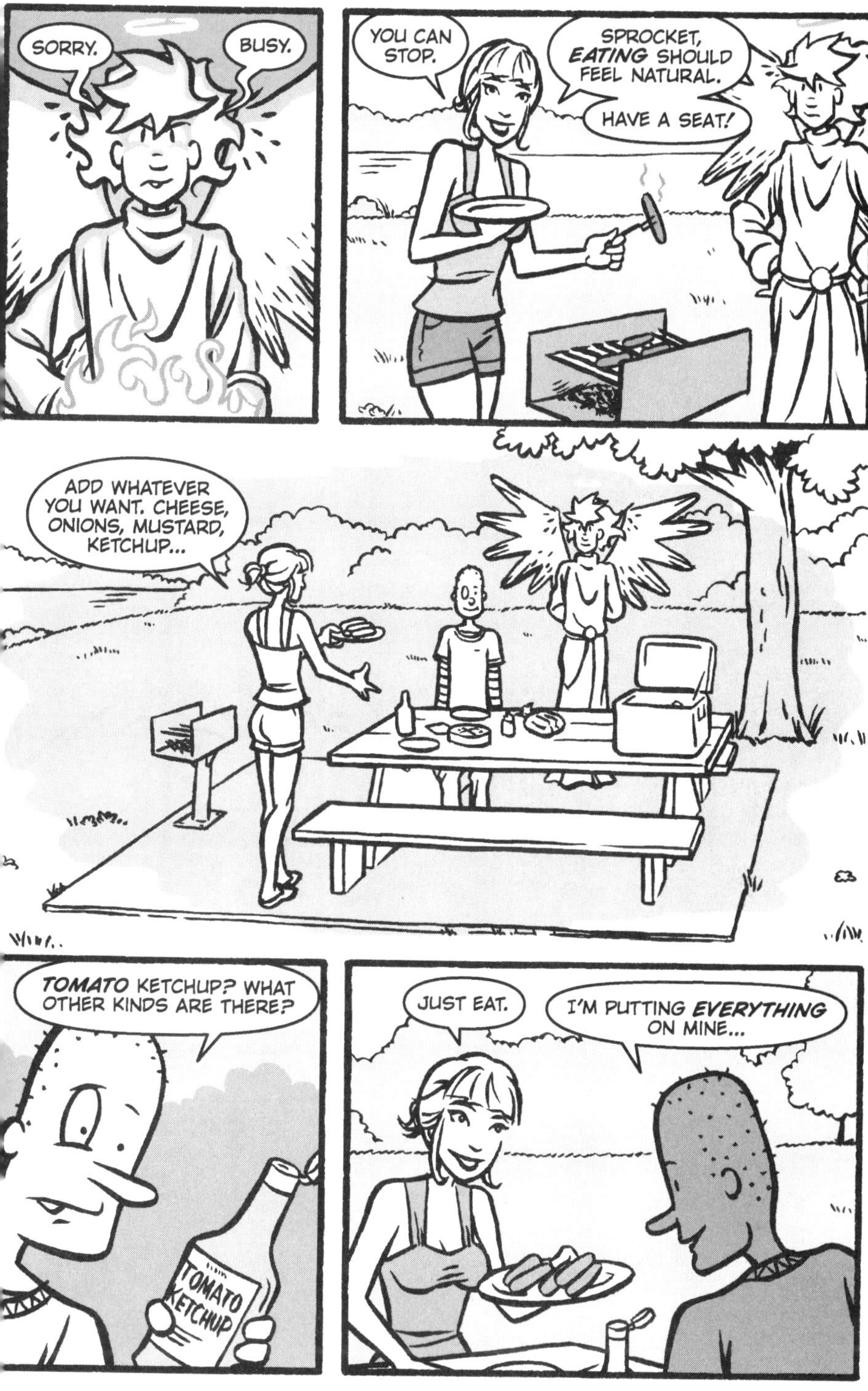
SORRY.
BUSY.
YOU CAN STOP.
SPROCKET, *EATING* SHOULD FEEL NATURAL.
HAVE A SEAT!
ADD WHATEVER YOU WANT. CHEESE, ONIONS, MUSTARD, KETCHUP...
TOMATO KETCHUP? WHAT OTHER KINDS ARE THERE?
TOMATO KETCHUP
JUST EAT.
I'M PUTTING *EVERYTHING* ON MINE...

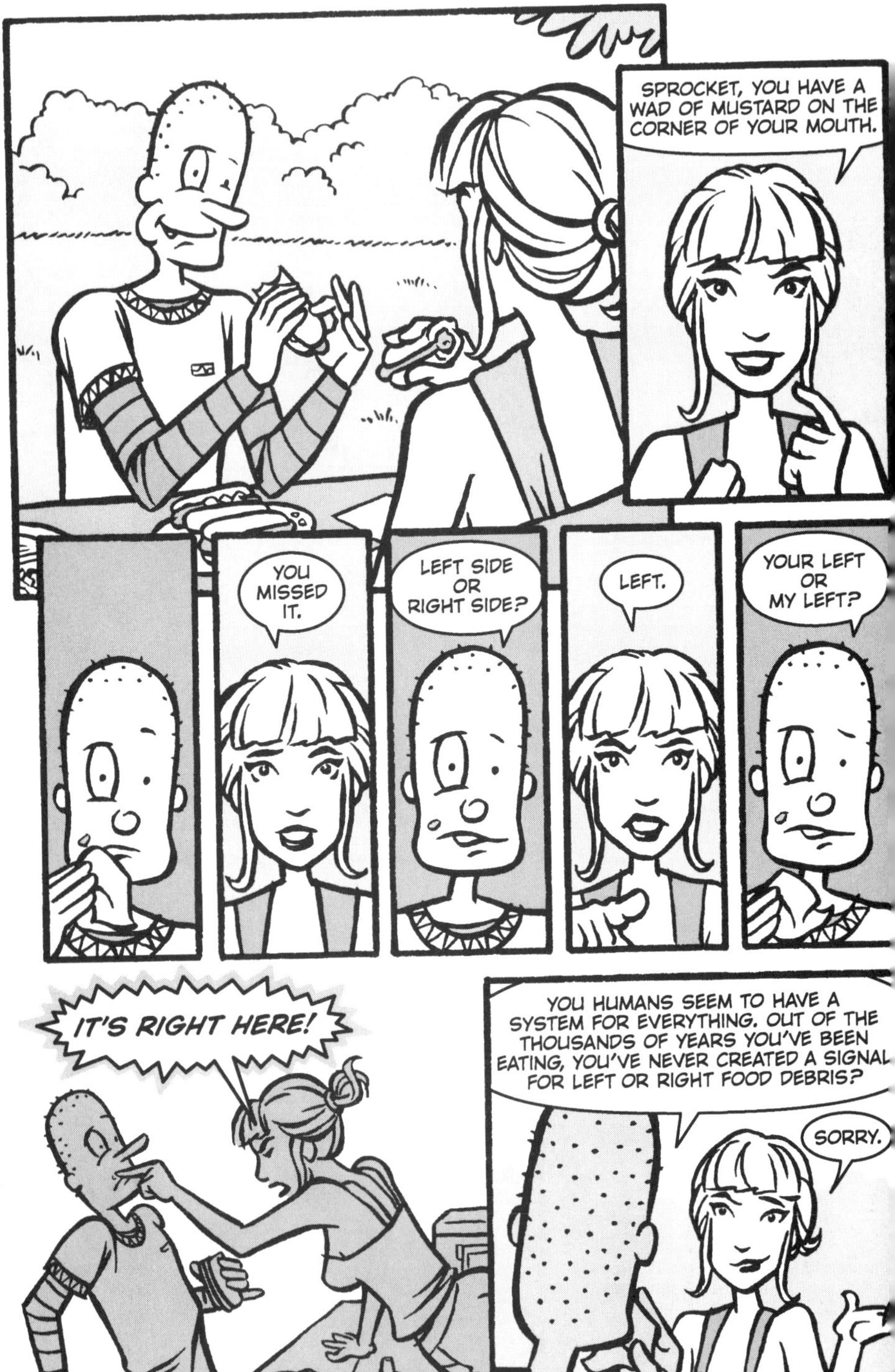
SPROCKET, YOU HAVE A WAD OF MUSTARD ON THE CORNER OF YOUR MOUTH.
YOU MISSED IT.
LEFT SIDE OR RIGHT SIDE?
LEFT.
YOUR LEFT OR MY LEFT?
IT'S RIGHT HERE!
YOU HUMANS SEEM TO HAVE A SYSTEM FOR EVERYTHING. OUT OF THE THOUSANDS OF YEARS YOU'VE BEEN EATING, YOU'VE NEVER CREATED A SIGNAL FOR LEFT OR RIGHT FOOD DEBRIS?
SORRY.

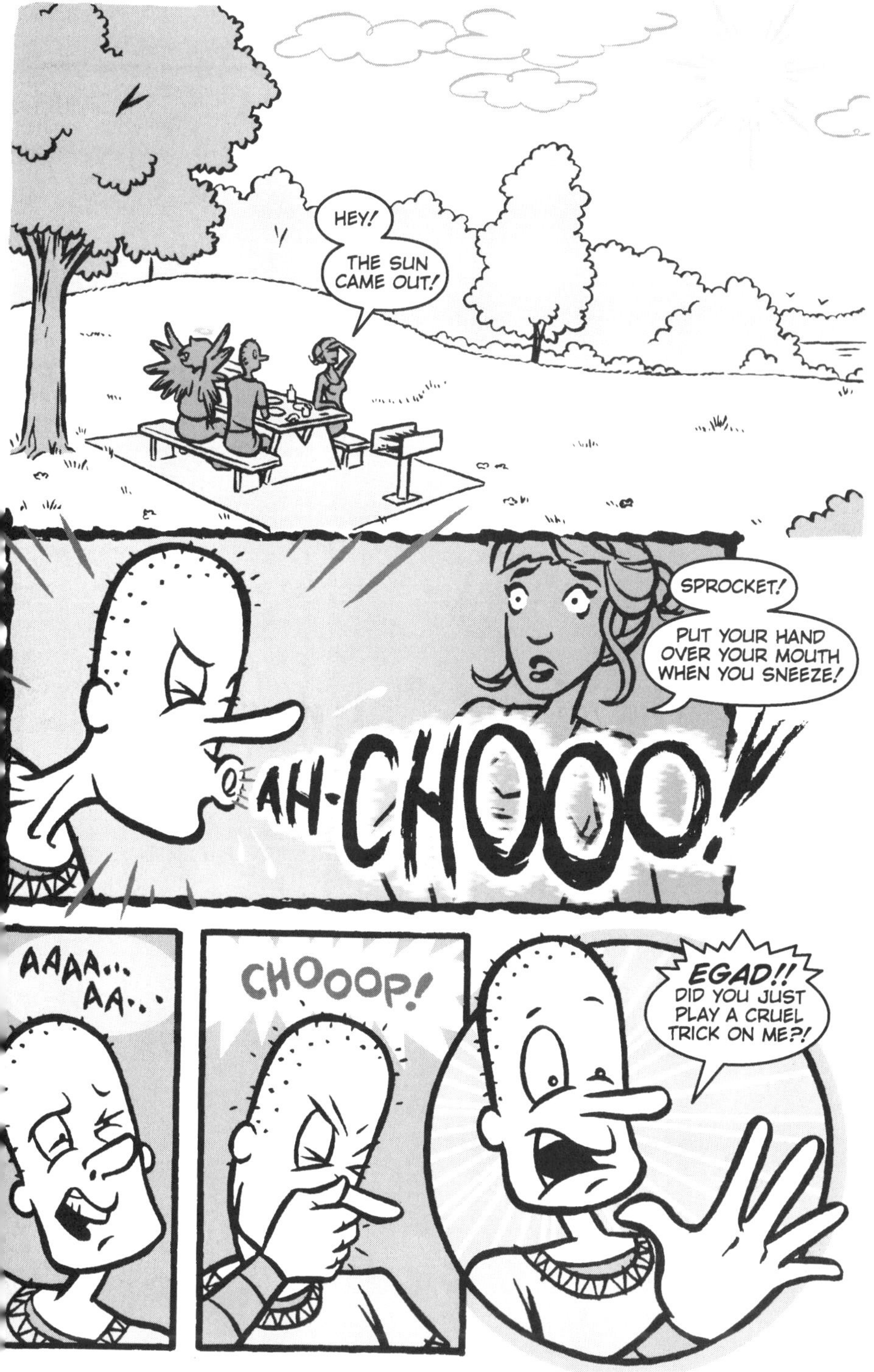
HEY!
THE SUN CAME OUT!
SPROCKET!
PUT YOUR HAND OVER YOUR MOUTH WHEN YOU SNEEZE!
AH-CHOOOO!
AAAA... AA...
CHOOOP!
EGAD!! DID YOU JUST PLAY A CRUEL TRICK ON ME?!

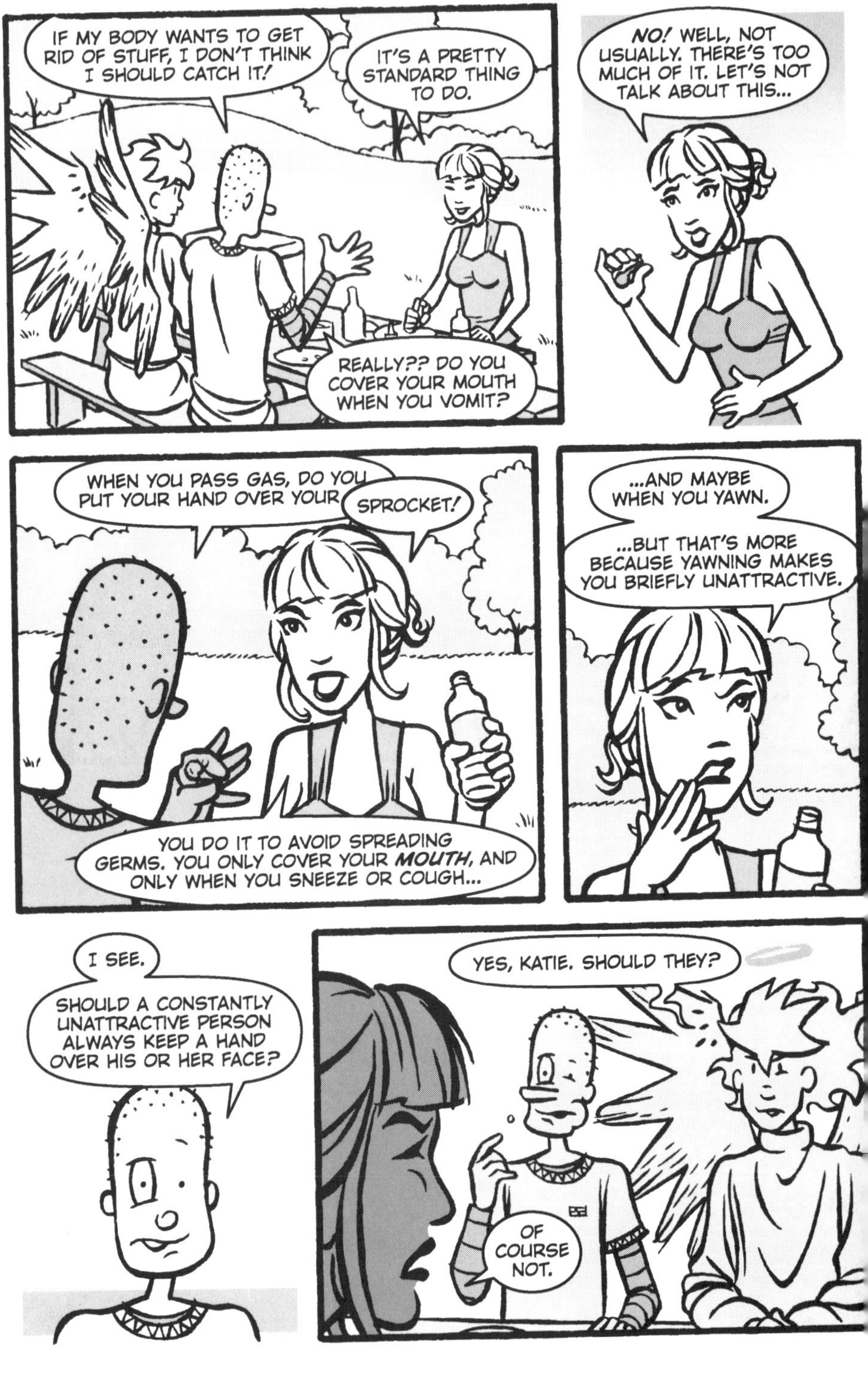

IF MY BODY WANTS TO GET RID OF STUFF, I DON'T THINK I SHOULD CATCH IT!
IT'S A PRETTY STANDARD THING TO DO.
REALLY?? DO YOU COVER YOUR MOUTH WHEN YOU VOMIT?
NO! WELL, NOT USUALLY. THERE'S TOO MUCH OF IT. LET'S NOT TALK ABOUT THIS...
WHEN YOU PASS GAS, DO YOU PUT YOUR HAND OVER YOUR
SPROCKET!
YOU DO IT TO AVOID SPREADING GERMS. YOU ONLY COVER YOUR MOUTH, AND ONLY WHEN YOU SNEEZE OR COUGH...
...AND MAYBE WHEN YOU YAWN.
...BUT THAT'S MORE BECAUSE YAWNING MAKES YOU BRIEFLY UNATTRACTIVE.
I SEE.
SHOULD A CONSTANTLY UNATTRACTIVE PERSON ALWAYS KEEP A HAND OVER HIS OR HER FACE?
YES, KATIE. SHOULD THEY?
OF COURSE NOT.

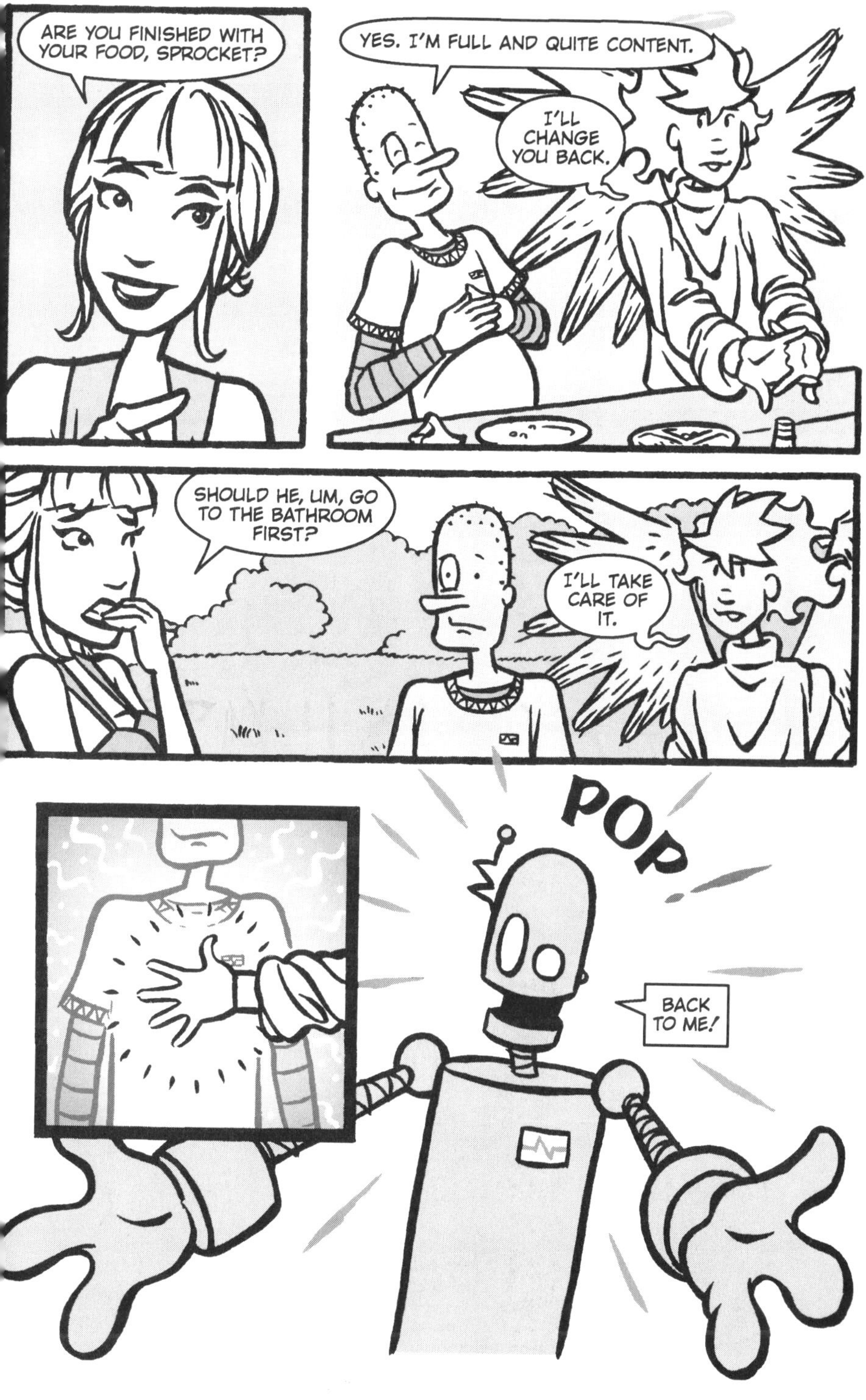
ARE YOU FINISHED WITH YOUR FOOD, SPROCKET?
YES. I'M FULL AND QUITE CONTENT.
I'LL CHANGE YOU BACK.
SHOULD HE, UM, GO TO THE BATHROOM FIRST?
I'LL TAKE CARE OF IT.
POP
BACK TO ME!

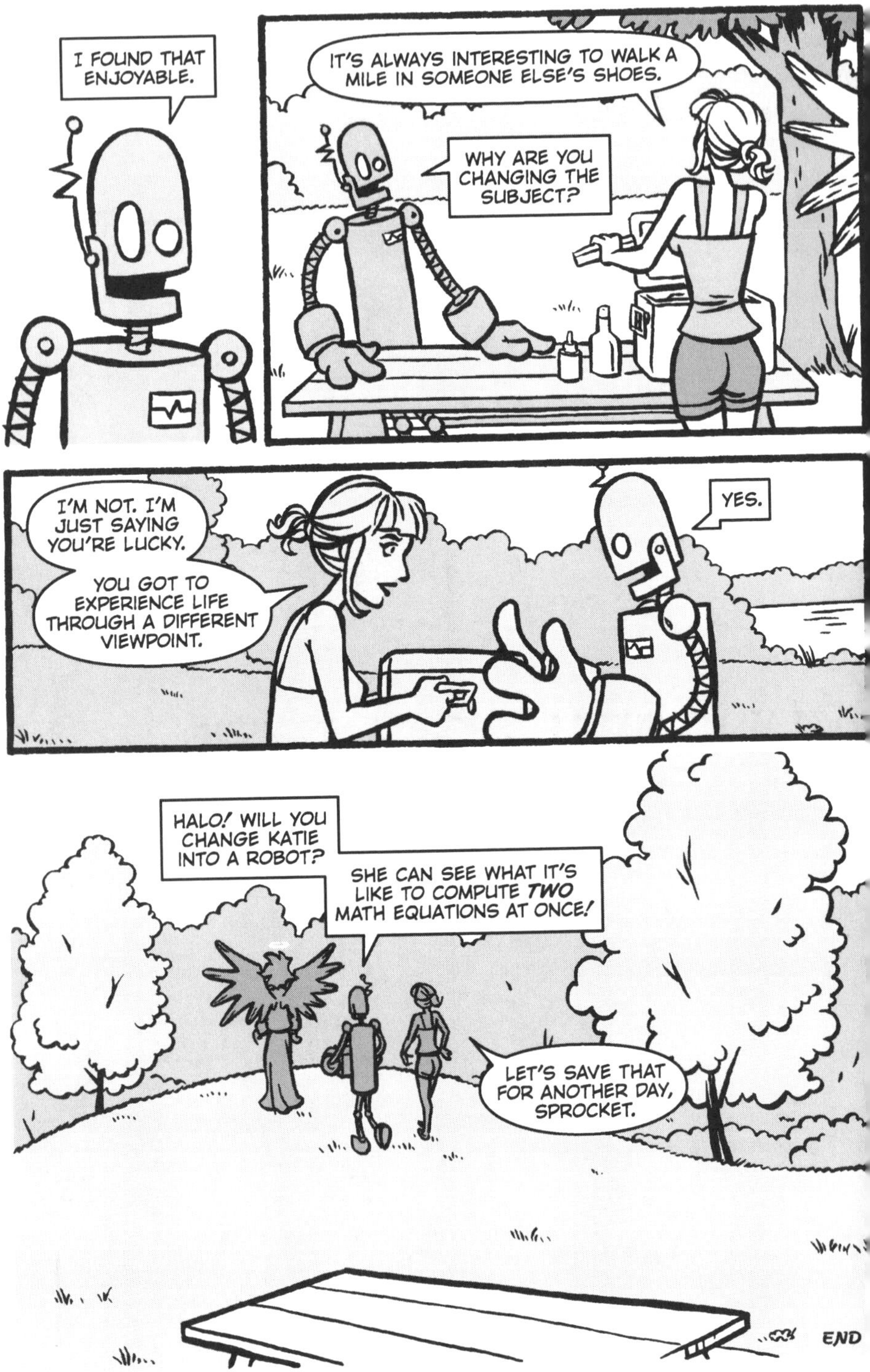
I FOUND THAT ENJOYABLE.
IT'S ALWAYS INTERESTING TO WALK A MILE IN SOMEONE ELSE'S SHOES.
WHY ARE YOU CHANGING THE SUBJECT?
I'M NOT. I'M JUST SAYING YOU'RE LUCKY.
YOU GOT TO EXPERIENCE LIFE THROUGH A DIFFERENT VIEWPOINT.
YES.
HALO! WILL YOU CHANGE KATIE INTO A ROBOT?
SHE CAN SEE WHAT IT'S LIKE TO COMPUTE *TWO* MATH EQUATIONS AT ONCE!
LET'S SAVE THAT FOR ANOTHER DAY, SPROCKET.
END

HALO AND SPROCKET

"CHEW ON THIS"

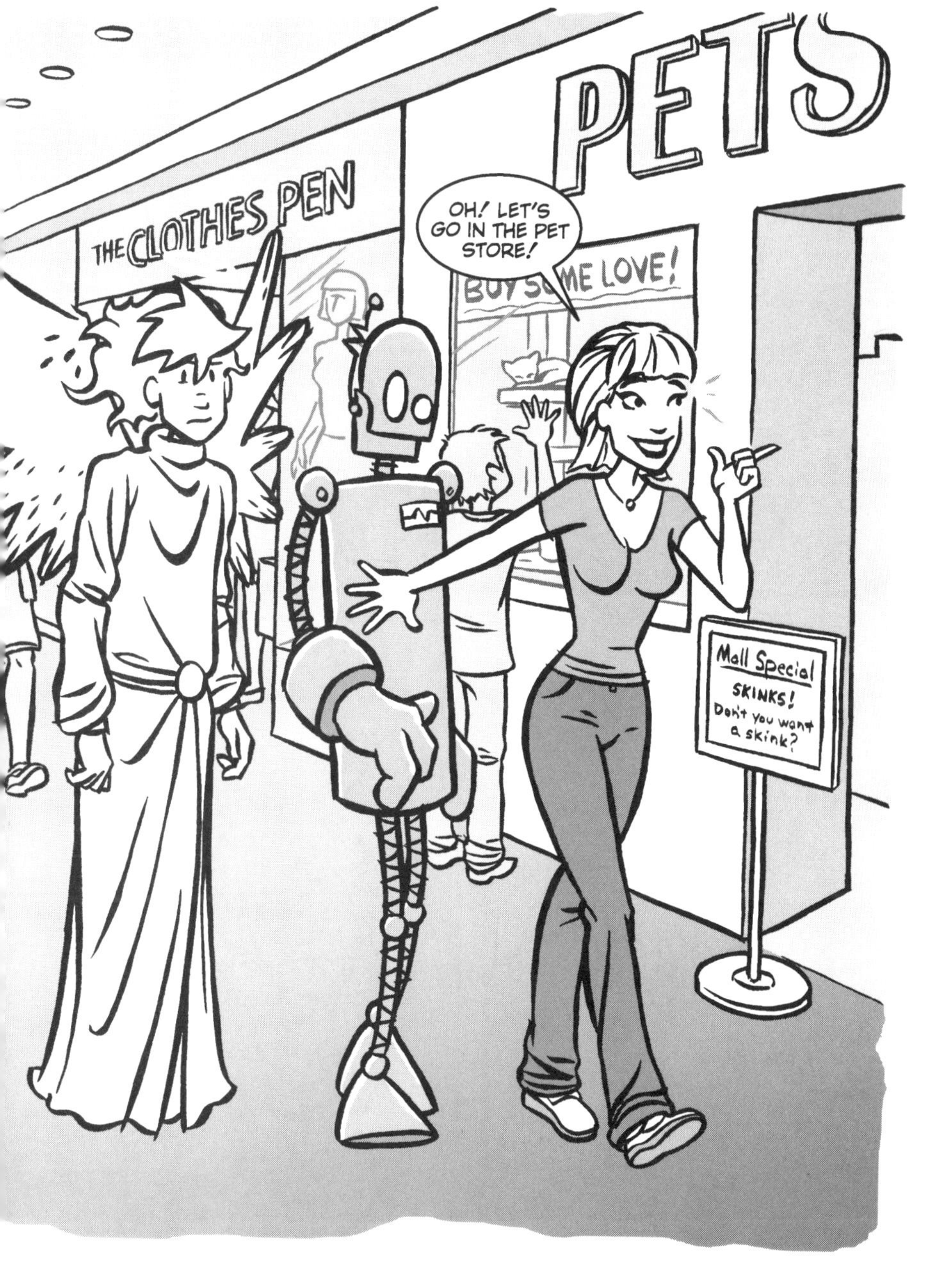

PETS
THE CLOTHES PEN
OH! LET'S GO IN THE PET STORE!
BUY S ME LOVE!
Mall Special
SKINKS!
Don't you want a skink?

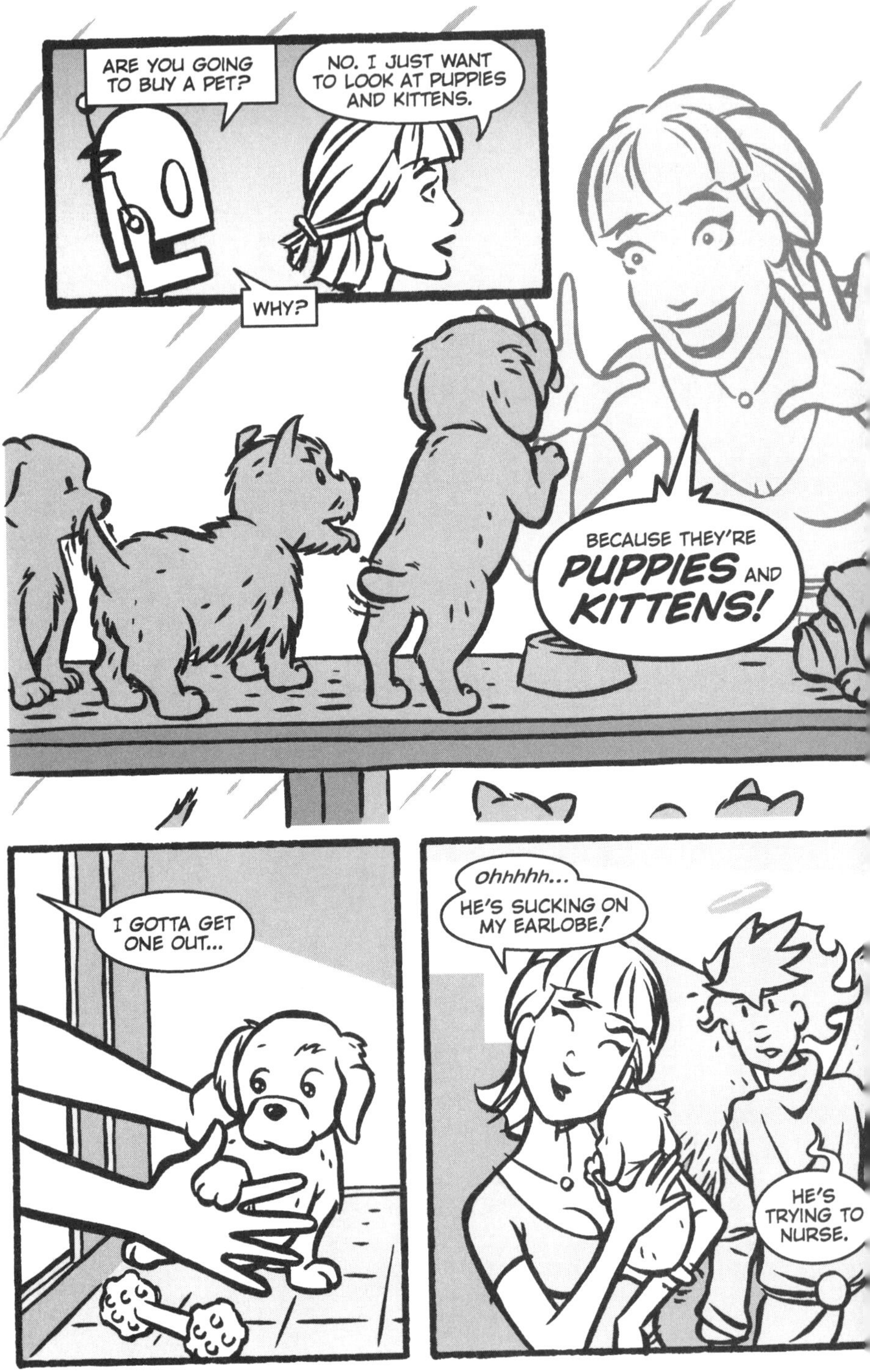
ARE YOU GOING TO BUY A PET?
NO. I JUST WANT TO LOOK AT PUPPIES AND KITTENS.
WHY?
BECAUSE THEY'RE PUPPIES AND KITTENS!
I GOTTA GET ONE OUT...
Ohhhhh... HE'S SUCKING ON MY EARLOBE!
HE'S TRYING TO NURSE.

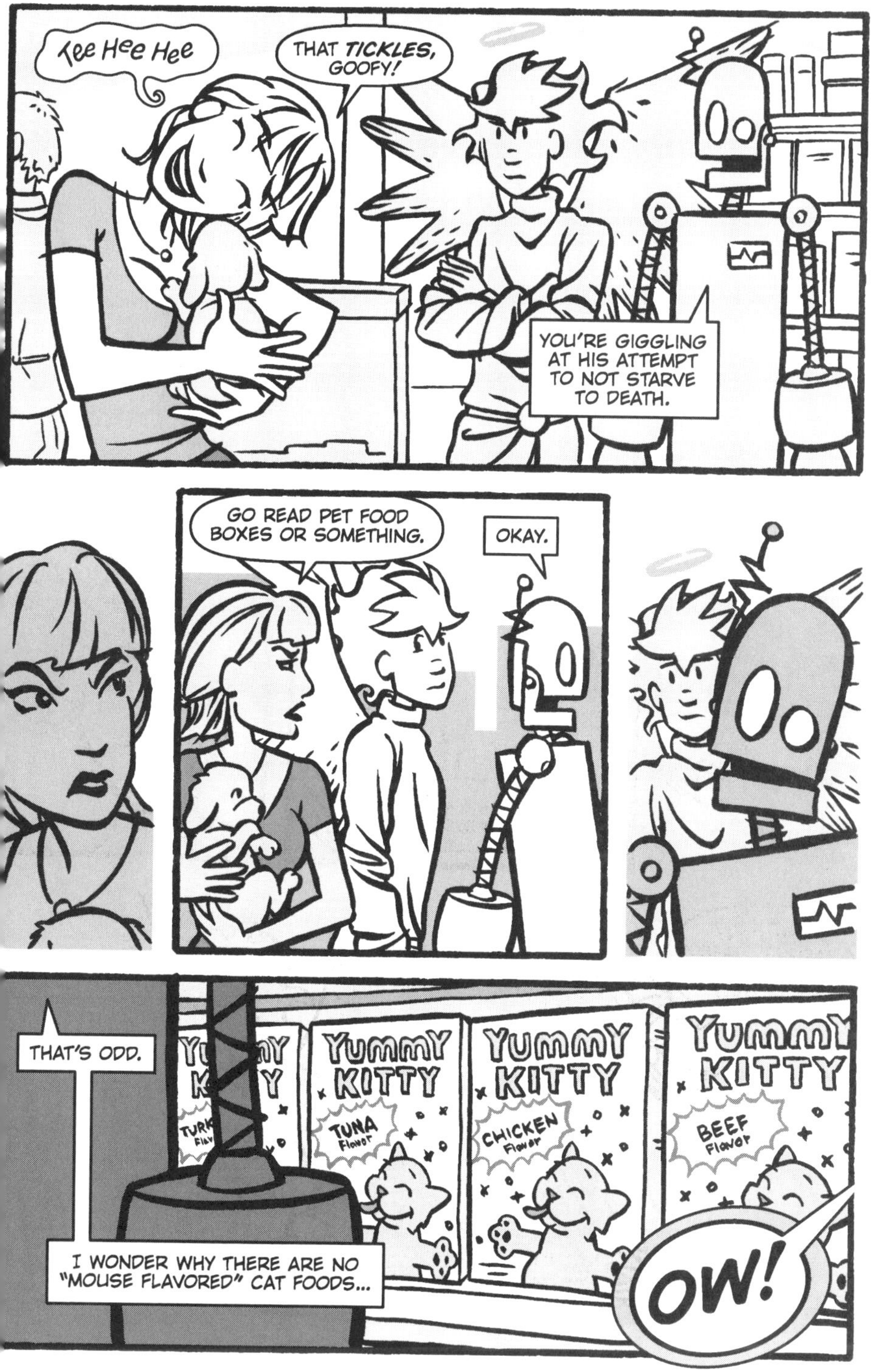
Tee Hee Hee
THAT TICKLES, GOOFY!
YOU'RE GIGGLING AT HIS ATTEMPT TO NOT STARVE TO DEATH.
GO READ PET FOOD BOXES OR SOMETHING.
OKAY.
THAT'S ODD.
YUMMY KITTY
TUNA Flavor
YUMMY KITTY
CHICKEN Flavor
YUMMY KITTY
BEEF Flavor
I WONDER WHY THERE ARE NO "MOUSE FLAVORED" CAT FOODS...
OW!

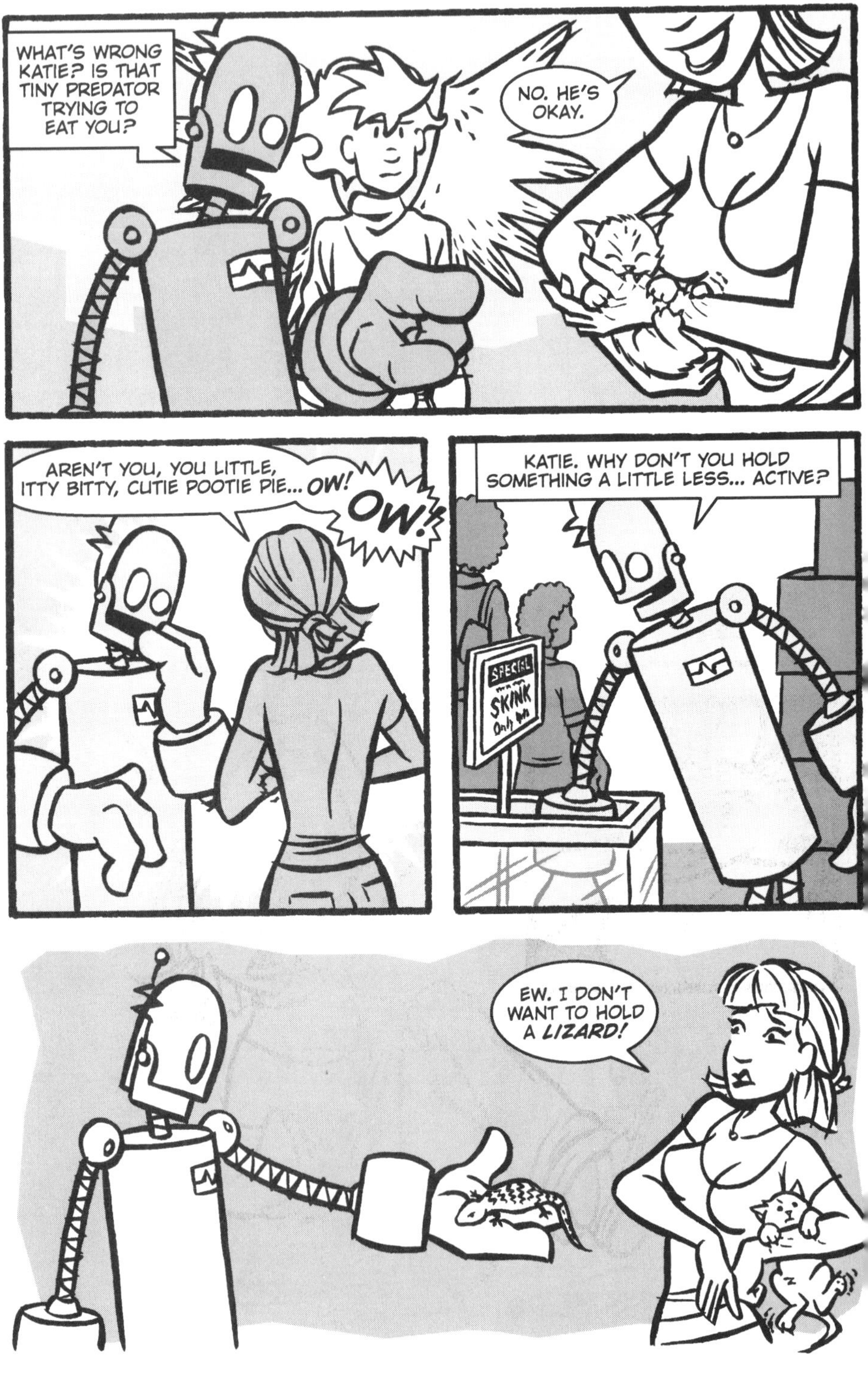
WHAT'S WRONG KATIE? IS THAT TINY PREDATOR TRYING TO EAT YOU?
NO. HE'S OKAY.
AREN'T YOU, YOU LITTLE, ITTY BITTY, CUTIE POOTIE PIE... OW!
OW!
KATIE. WHY DON'T YOU HOLD SOMETHING A LITTLE LESS... ACTIVE?
SPECIAL
SKINK
EW. I DON'T WANT TO HOLD A LIZARD!

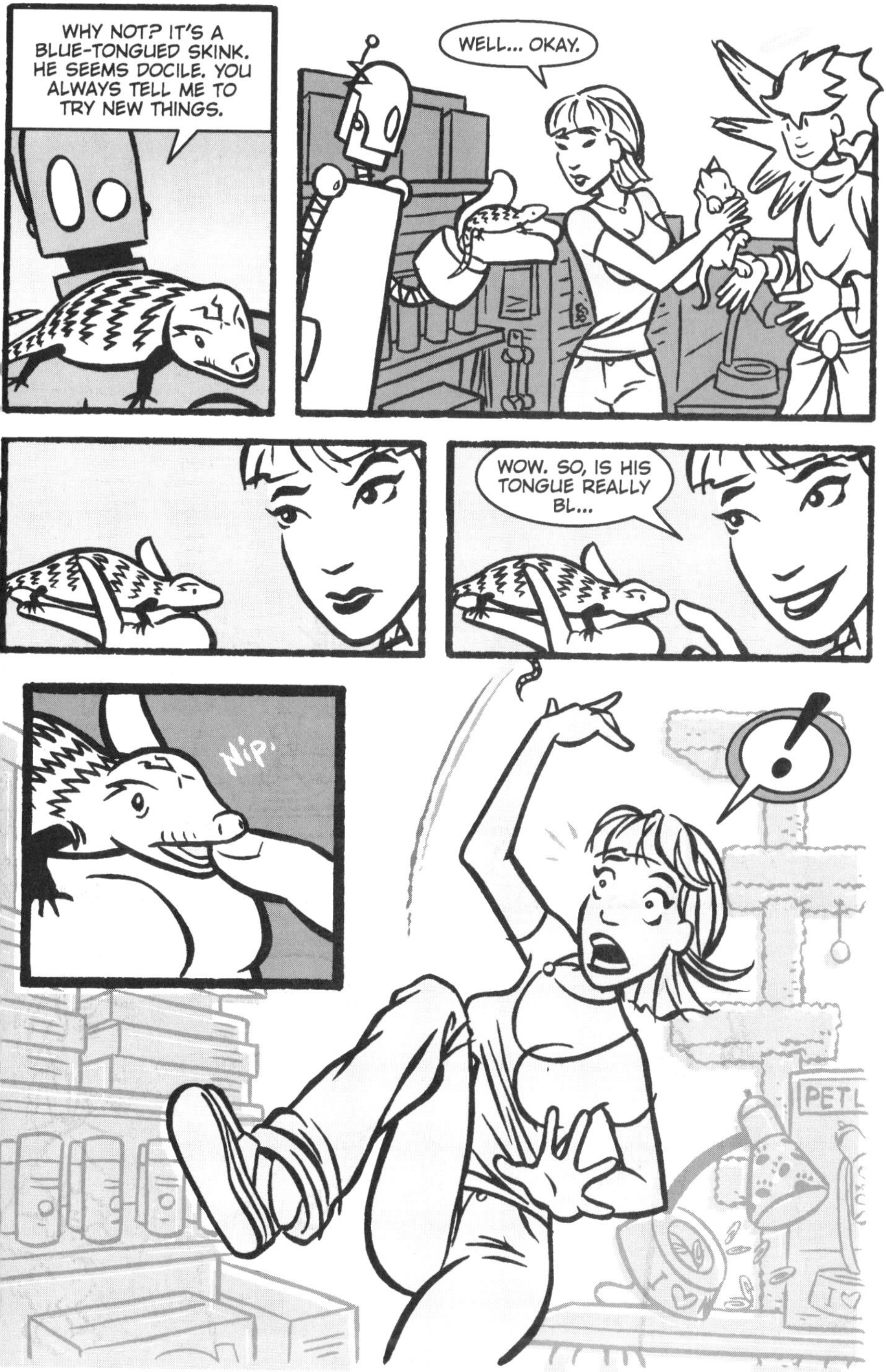
WHY NOT? IT'S A BLUE-TONGUED SKINK. HE SEEMS DOCILE. YOU ALWAYS TELL ME TO TRY NEW THINGS.
WELL... OKAY.
WOW. SO, IS HIS TONGUE REALLY BL...
NIP!
!
PET

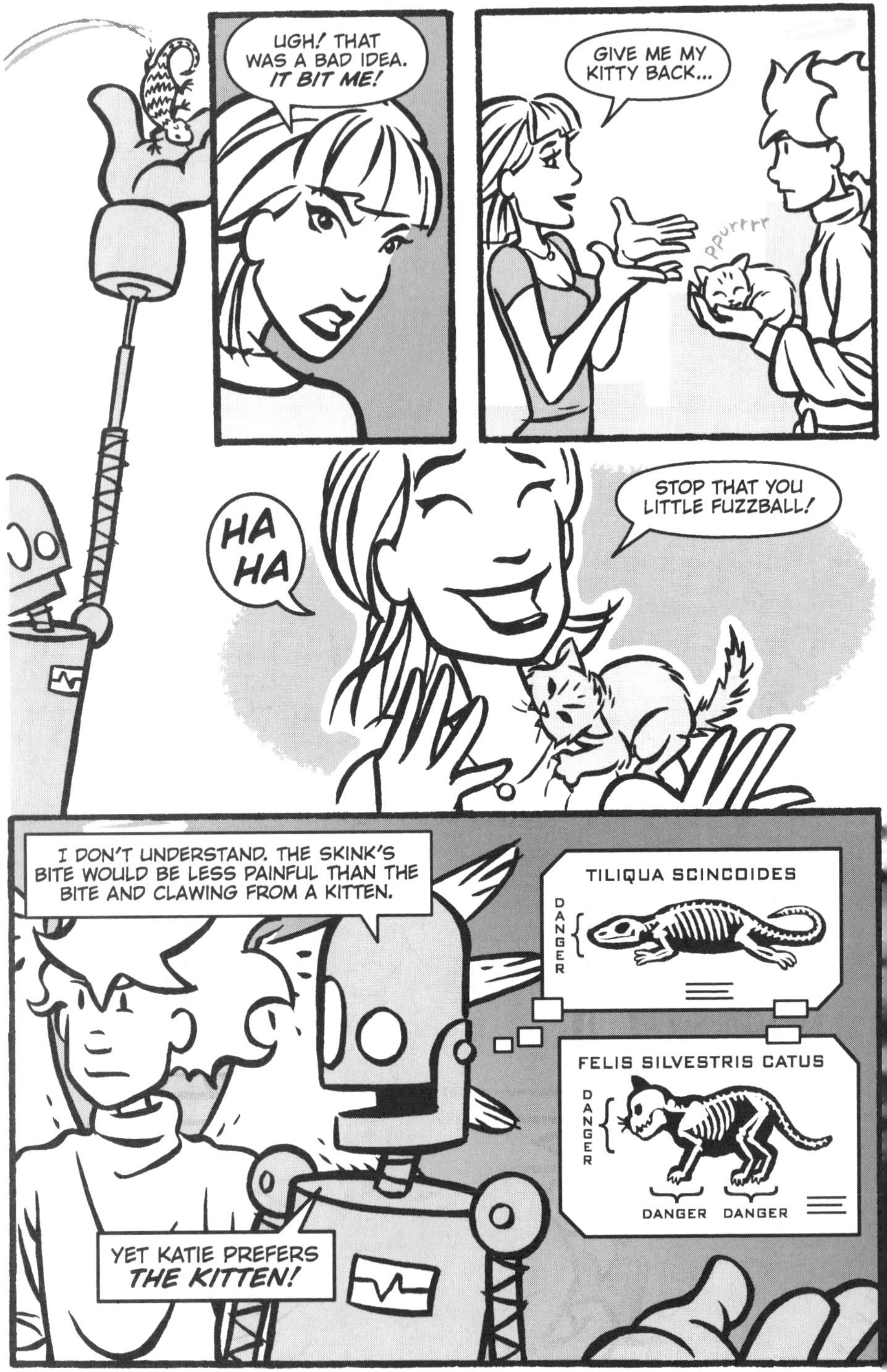
UGH! THAT WAS A BAD IDEA. IT BIT ME!
GIVE ME MY KITTY BACK...
PPURRRR
HA HA
STOP THAT YOU LITTLE FUZZBALL!
I DON'T UNDERSTAND. THE SKINK'S BITE WOULD BE LESS PAINFUL THAN THE BITE AND CLAWING FROM A KITTEN.
TILIQUA SCINCOIDES
DANGER
FELIS SILVESTRIS CATUS
DANGER
DANGER DANGER
YET KATIE PREFERS THE KITTEN!

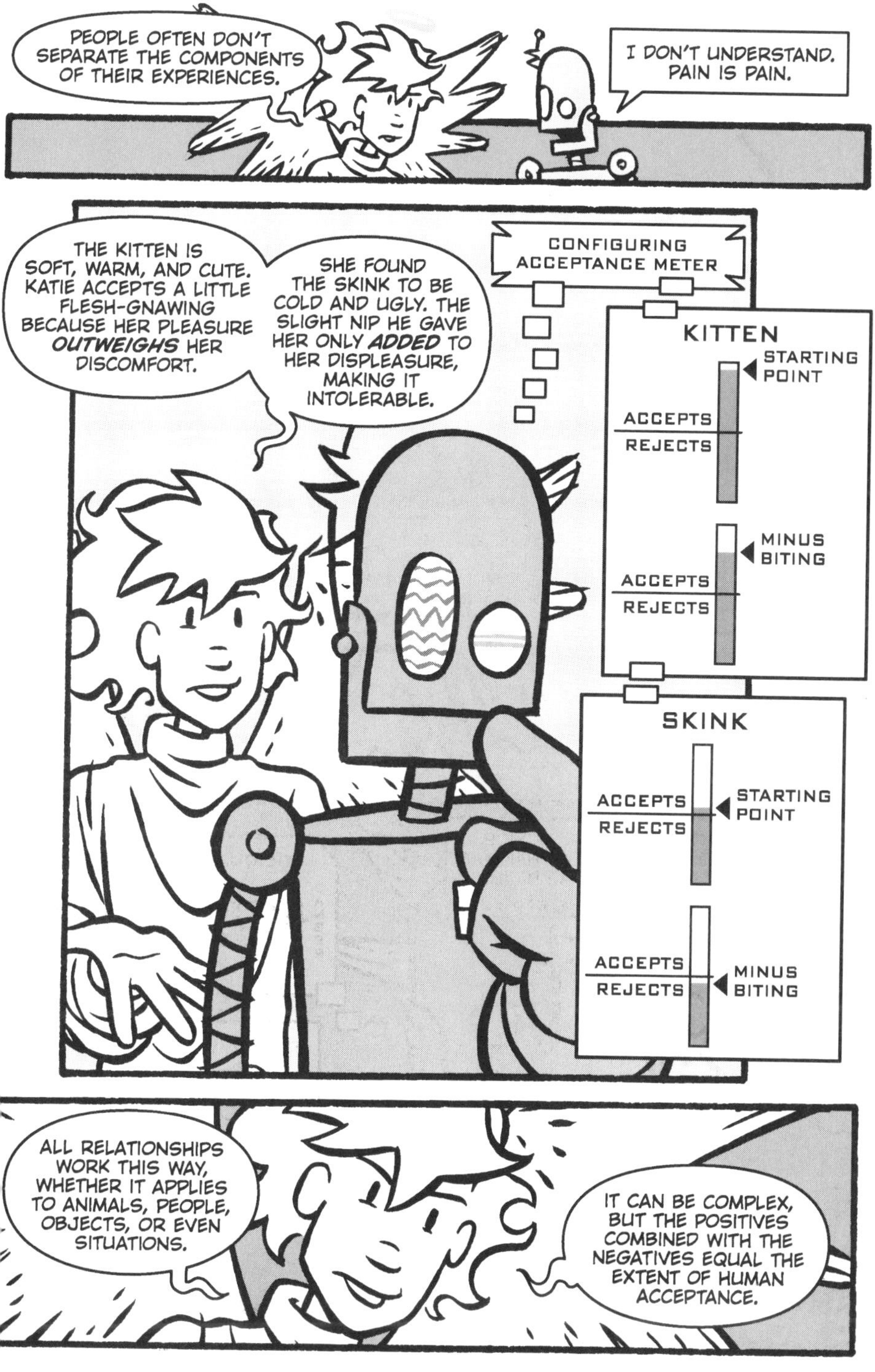
PEOPLE OFTEN DON'T SEPARATE THE COMPONENTS OF THEIR EXPERIENCES.
I DON'T UNDERSTAND. PAIN IS PAIN.
THE KITTEN IS SOFT, WARM, AND CUTE. KATIE ACCEPTS A LITTLE FLESH-GNAWING BECAUSE HER PLEASURE OUTWEIGHS HER DISCOMFORT.
SHE FOUND THE SKINK TO BE COLD AND UGLY. THE SLIGHT NIP HE GAVE HER ONLY ADDED TO HER DISPLEASURE, MAKING IT INTOLERABLE.
CONFIGURING ACCEPTANCE METER
KITTEN
STARTING POINT
ACCEPTS
REJECTS
MINUS BITING
ACCEPTS
REJECTS
SKINK
ACCEPTS
REJECTS
STARTING POINT
ACCEPTS
REJECTS
MINUS BITING
ALL RELATIONSHIPS WORK THIS WAY, WHETHER IT APPLIES TO ANIMALS, PEOPLE, OBJECTS, OR EVEN SITUATIONS.
IT CAN BE COMPLEX, BUT THE POSITIVES COMBINED WITH THE NEGATIVES EQUAL THE EXTENT OF HUMAN ACCEPTANCE.

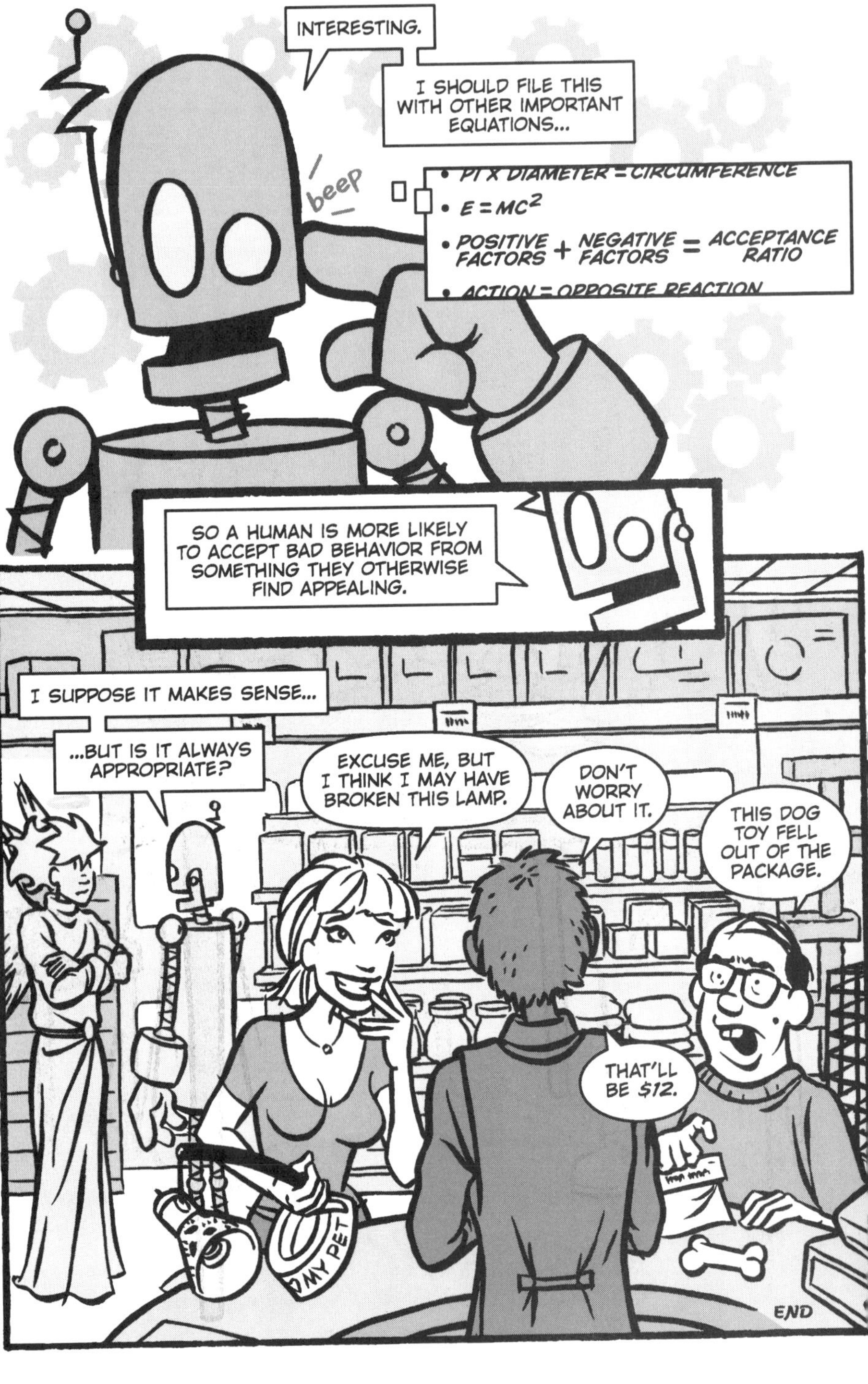
INTERESTING.
I SHOULD FILE THIS WITH OTHER IMPORTANT EQUATIONS...
beep
• PI X DIAMETER = CIRCUMFERENCE
• E = MC²
• POSITIVE FACTORS + NEGATIVE FACTORS = ACCEPTANCE RATIO
• ACTION = OPPOSITE REACTION
SO A HUMAN IS MORE LIKELY TO ACCEPT BAD BEHAVIOR FROM SOMETHING THEY OTHERWISE FIND APPEALING.
I SUPPOSE IT MAKES SENSE...
...BUT IS IT ALWAYS APPROPRIATE?
EXCUSE ME, BUT I THINK I MAY HAVE BROKEN THIS LAMP.
DON'T WORRY ABOUT IT.
THIS DOG TOY FELL OUT OF THE PACKAGE.
THAT'LL BE $12.
MY PET
END

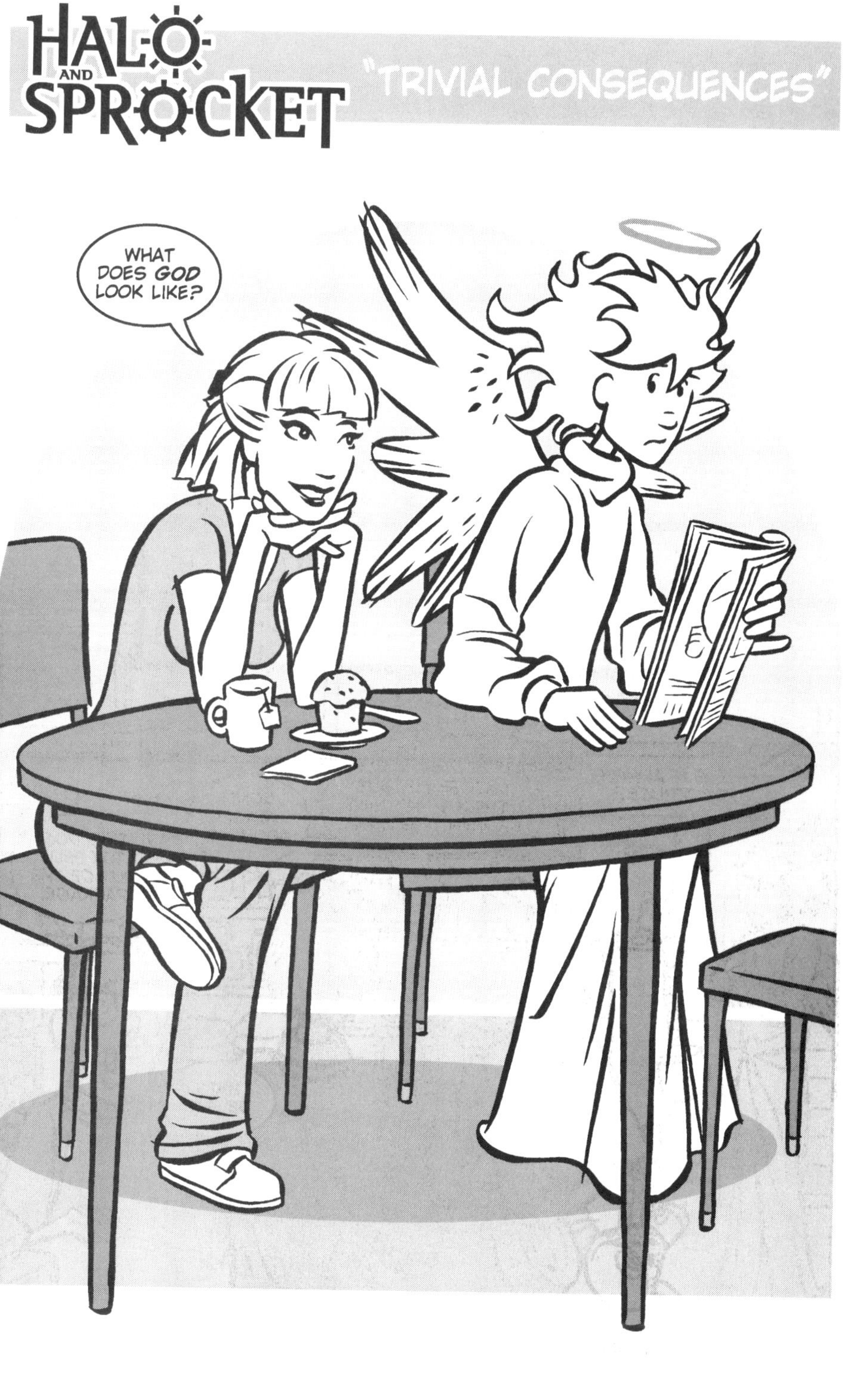
HALO AND SPROCKET
"TRIVIAL CONSEQUENCES"
WHAT DOES GOD LOOK LIKE?

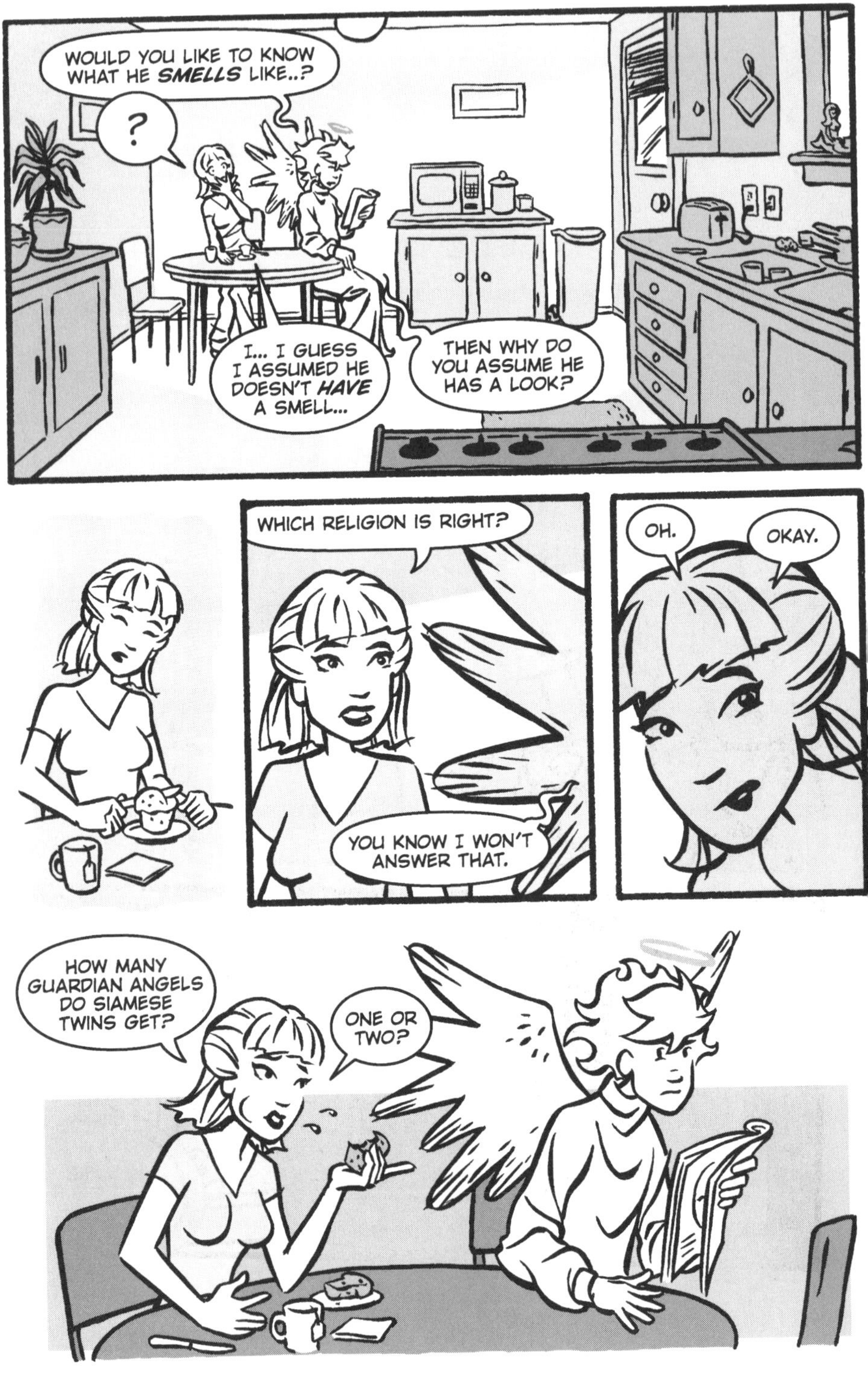
WOULD YOU LIKE TO KNOW WHAT HE SMELLS LIKE..?
?
I... I GUESS I ASSUMED HE DOESN'T HAVE A SMELL...
THEN WHY DO YOU ASSUME HE HAS A LOOK?
WHICH RELIGION IS RIGHT?
YOU KNOW I WON'T ANSWER THAT.
OH.
OKAY.
HOW MANY GUARDIAN ANGELS DO SIAMESE TWINS GET?
ONE OR TWO?

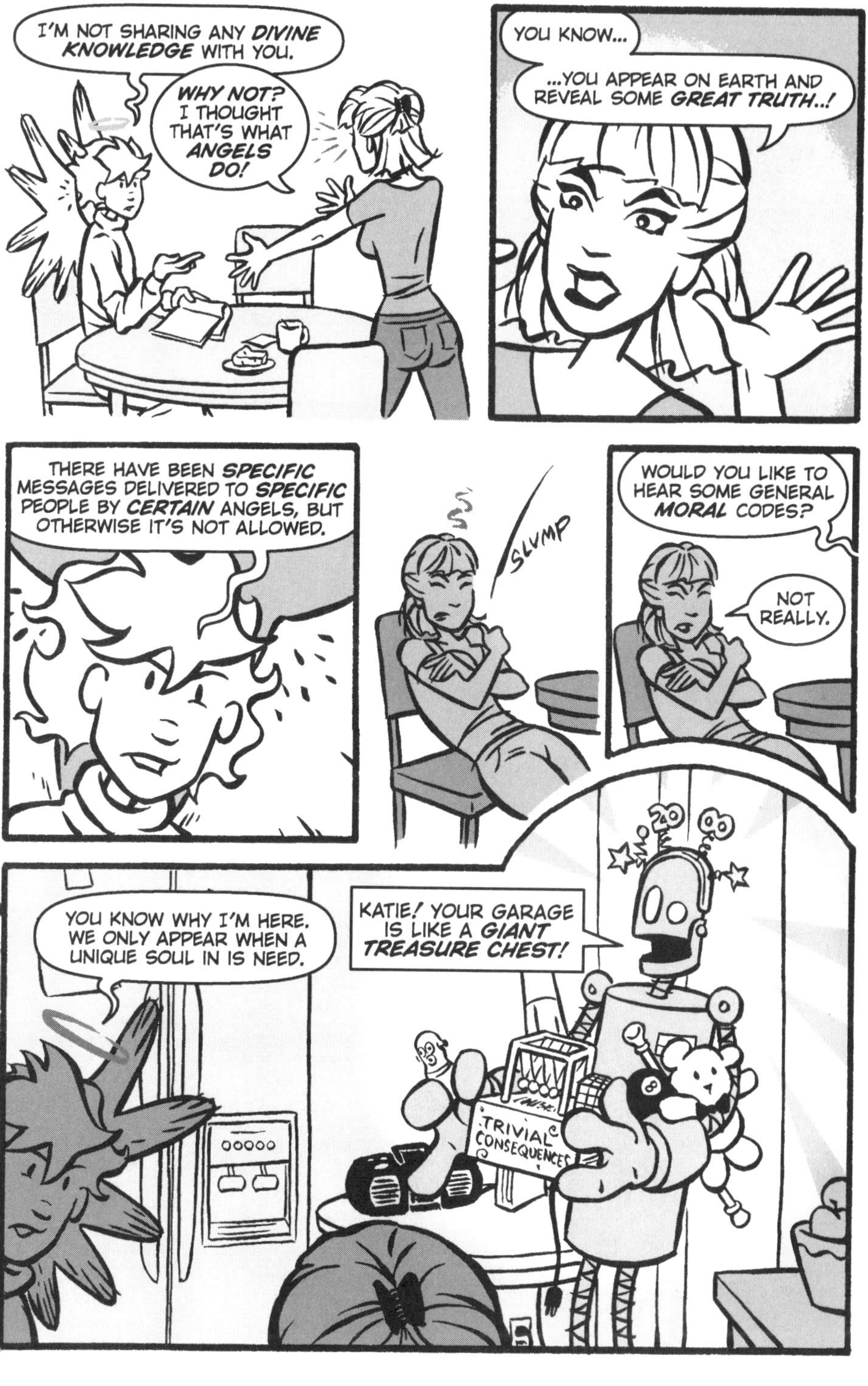
I'M NOT SHARING ANY DIVINE KNOWLEDGE WITH YOU.
WHY NOT? I THOUGHT THAT'S WHAT ANGELS DO!
YOU KNOW...
...YOU APPEAR ON EARTH AND REVEAL SOME GREAT TRUTH..!
THERE HAVE BEEN SPECIFIC MESSAGES DELIVERED TO SPECIFIC PEOPLE BY CERTAIN ANGELS, BUT OTHERWISE IT'S NOT ALLOWED.
SLUMP
WOULD YOU LIKE TO HEAR SOME GENERAL MORAL CODES?
NOT REALLY.
YOU KNOW WHY I'M HERE. WE ONLY APPEAR WHEN A UNIQUE SOUL IN IS NEED.
KATIE! YOUR GARAGE IS LIKE A GIANT TREASURE CHEST!
TRIVIAL CONSEQUENCES

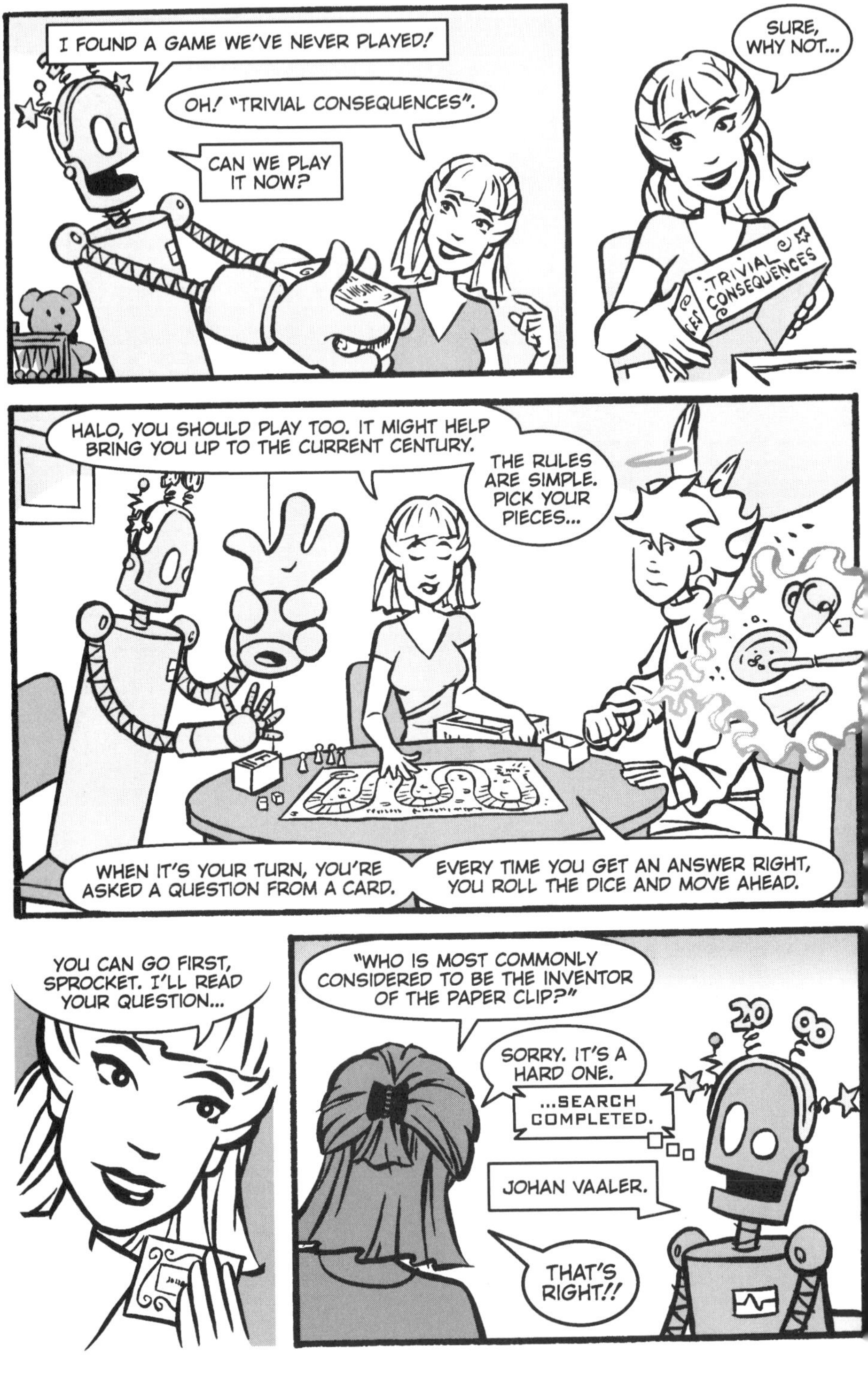
I FOUND A GAME WE'VE NEVER PLAYED!
OH! "TRIVIAL CONSEQUENCES".
CAN WE PLAY IT NOW?
SURE, WHY NOT...
TRIVIAL CONSEQUENCES
HALO, YOU SHOULD PLAY TOO. IT MIGHT HELP BRING YOU UP TO THE CURRENT CENTURY.
THE RULES ARE SIMPLE. PICK YOUR PIECES...
WHEN IT'S YOUR TURN, YOU'RE ASKED A QUESTION FROM A CARD.
EVERY TIME YOU GET AN ANSWER RIGHT, YOU ROLL THE DICE AND MOVE AHEAD.
YOU CAN GO FIRST, SPROCKET. I'LL READ YOUR QUESTION...
"WHO IS MOST COMMONLY CONSIDERED TO BE THE INVENTOR OF THE PAPER CLIP?"
SORRY. IT'S A HARD ONE.
...SEARCH COMPLETED.
JOHAN VAALER.
THAT'S RIGHT!!

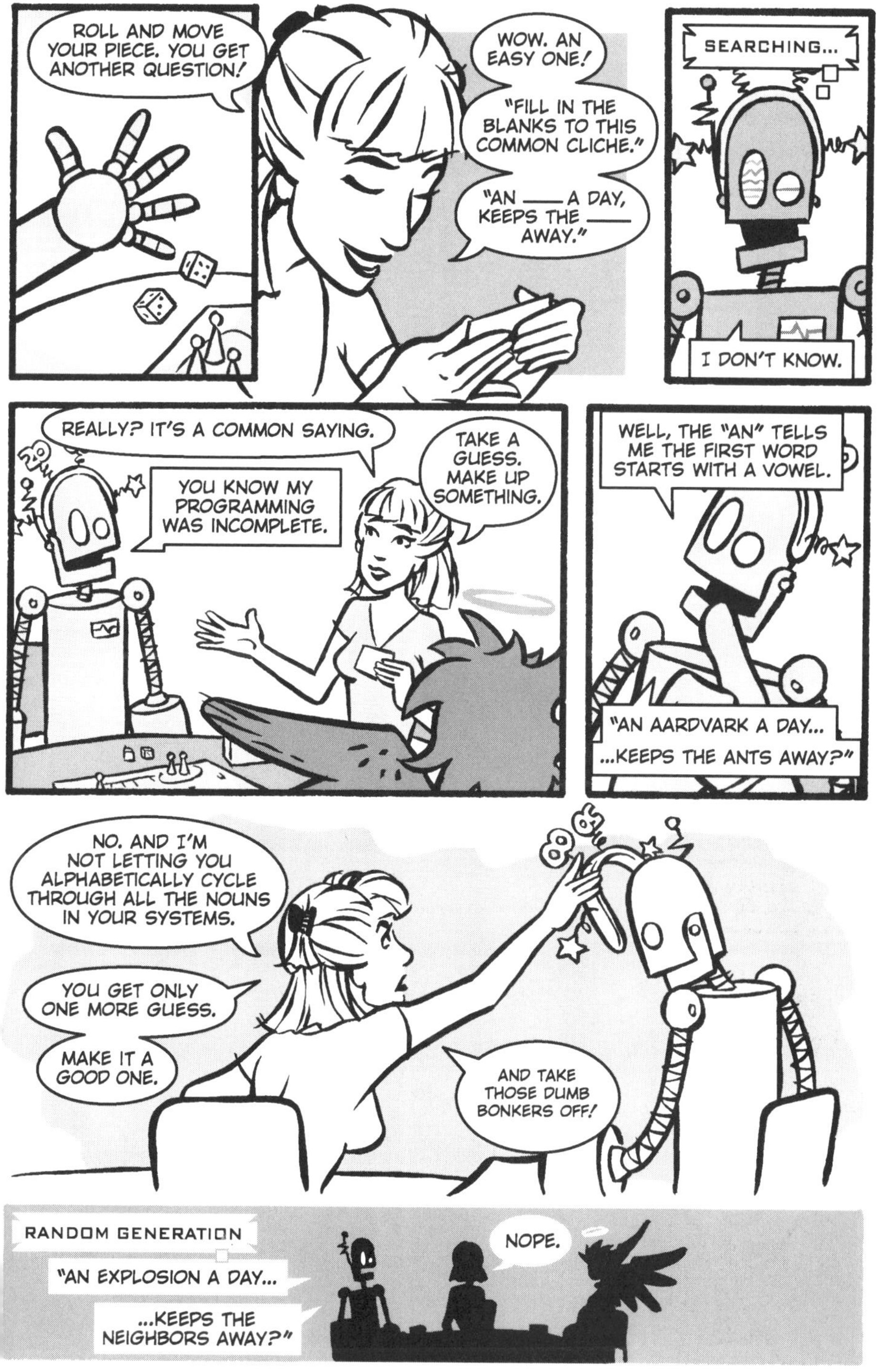
ROLL AND MOVE YOUR PIECE. YOU GET ANOTHER QUESTION!
WOW. AN EASY ONE!
"FILL IN THE BLANKS TO THIS COMMON CLICHE."
"AN ___ A DAY, KEEPS THE ___ AWAY."
SEARCHING...
I DON'T KNOW.
REALLY? IT'S A COMMON SAYING.
YOU KNOW MY PROGRAMMING WAS INCOMPLETE.
TAKE A GUESS. MAKE UP SOMETHING.
WELL, THE "AN" TELLS ME THE FIRST WORD STARTS WITH A VOWEL.
"AN AARDVARK A DAY...
...KEEPS THE ANTS AWAY?"
NO. AND I'M NOT LETTING YOU ALPHABETICALLY CYCLE THROUGH ALL THE NOUNS IN YOUR SYSTEMS.
YOU GET ONLY ONE MORE GUESS.
MAKE IT A GOOD ONE.
AND TAKE THOSE DUMB BONKERS OFF!
RANDOM GENERATION
"AN EXPLOSION A DAY...
...KEEPS THE NEIGHBORS AWAY?"
NOPE.

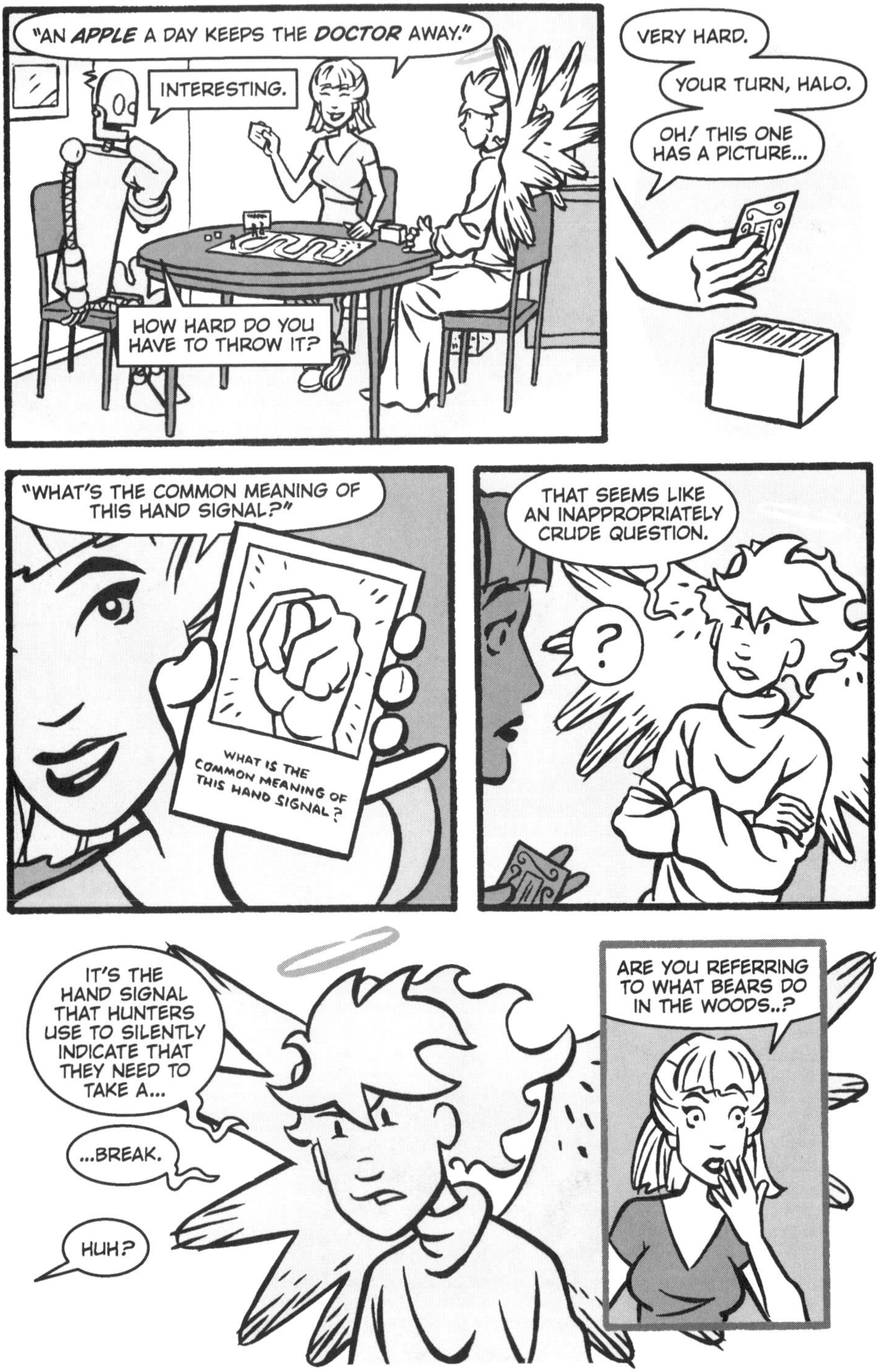
"AN APPLE A DAY KEEPS THE DOCTOR AWAY."
INTERESTING.
HOW HARD DO YOU HAVE TO THROW IT?
VERY HARD.
YOUR TURN, HALO.
OH! THIS ONE HAS A PICTURE...
"WHAT'S THE COMMON MEANING OF THIS HAND SIGNAL?"
WHAT IS THE COMMON MEANING OF THIS HAND SIGNAL?
THAT SEEMS LIKE AN INAPPROPRIATELY CRUDE QUESTION.
?
IT'S THE HAND SIGNAL THAT HUNTERS USE TO SILENTLY INDICATE THAT THEY NEED TO TAKE A...
...BREAK.
HUH?
ARE YOU REFERRING TO WHAT BEARS DO IN THE WOODS..?

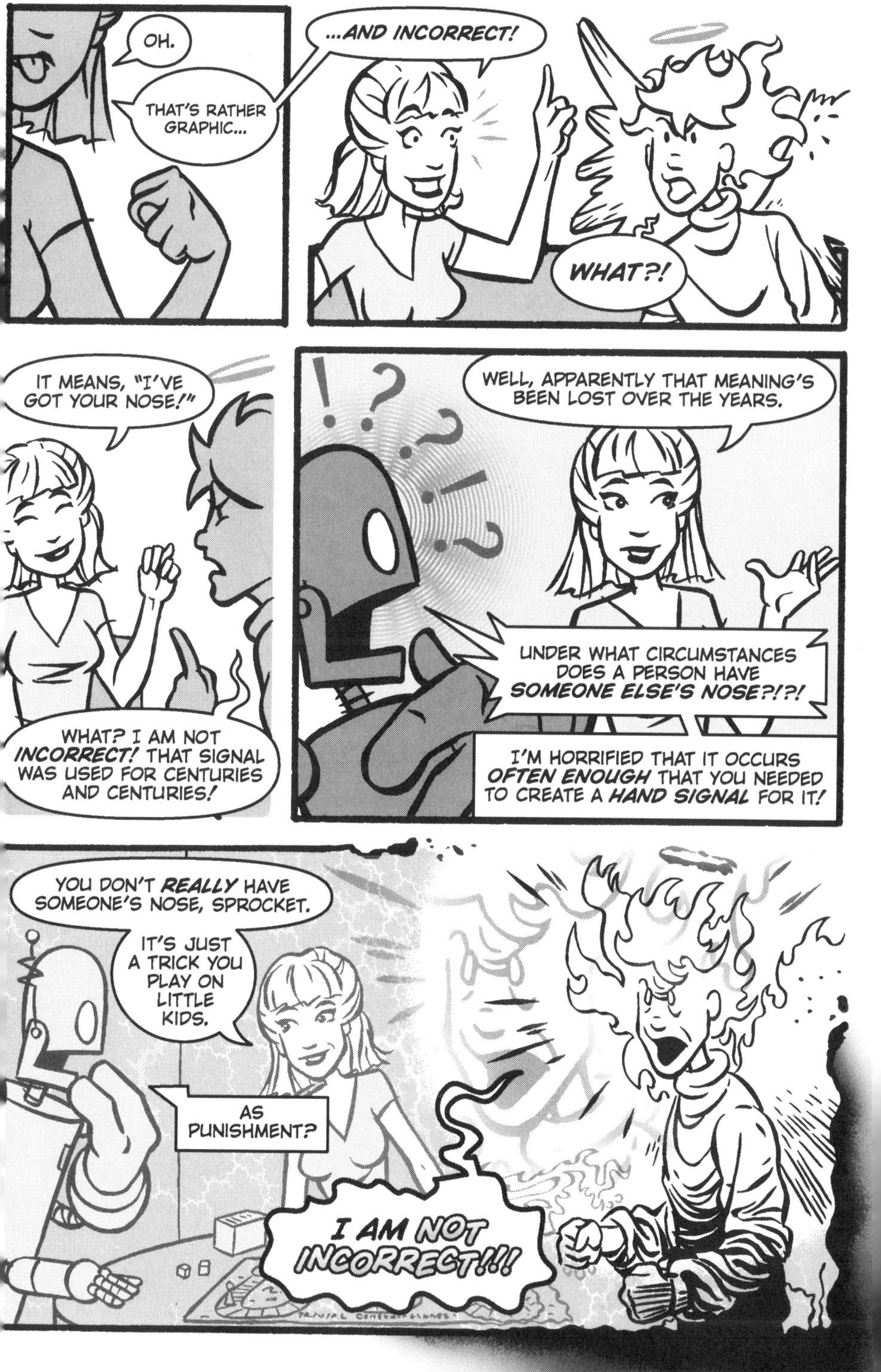
OH.
THAT'S RATHER GRAPHIC...
...AND INCORRECT!
WHAT?!
IT MEANS, "I'VE GOT YOUR NOSE!"
WHAT? I AM NOT *INCORRECT!* THAT SIGNAL WAS USED FOR CENTURIES AND CENTURIES!
WELL, APPARENTLY THAT MEANING'S BEEN LOST OVER THE YEARS.
UNDER WHAT CIRCUMSTANCES DOES A PERSON HAVE *SOMEONE ELSE'S NOSE?!?!*
I'M HORRIFIED THAT IT OCCURS *OFTEN ENOUGH* THAT YOU NEEDED TO CREATE A *HAND SIGNAL* FOR IT!
YOU DON'T *REALLY* HAVE SOMEONE'S NOSE, SPROCKET.
IT'S JUST A TRICK YOU PLAY ON LITTLE KIDS.
AS PUNISHMENT?
I AM NOT INCORRECT!!!

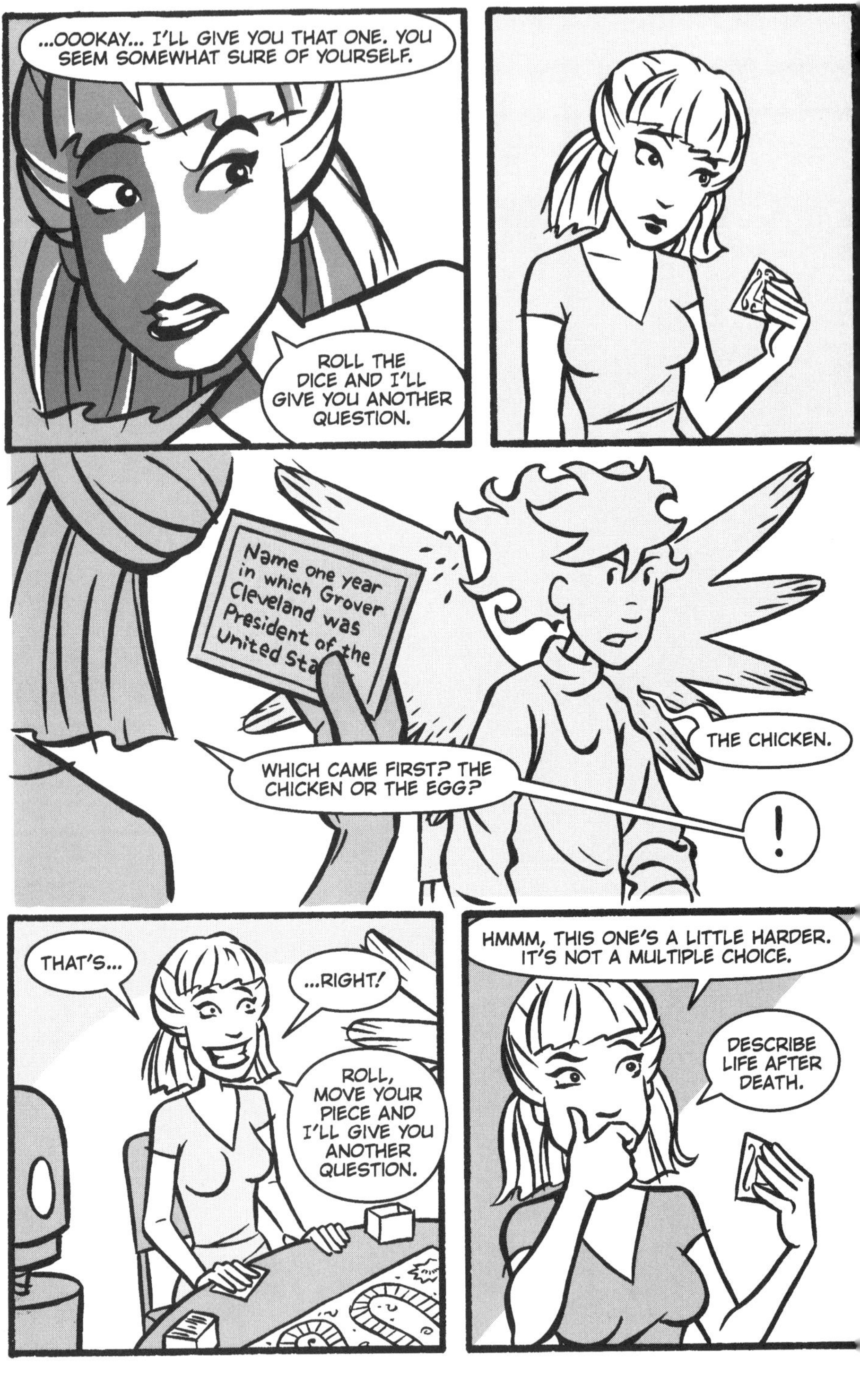
...OOOKAY... I'LL GIVE YOU THAT ONE. YOU SEEM SOMEWHAT SURE OF YOURSELF.
ROLL THE DICE AND I'LL GIVE YOU ANOTHER QUESTION.
Name one year in which Grover Cleveland was President of the United Sta
WHICH CAME FIRST? THE CHICKEN OR THE EGG?
THE CHICKEN.
!
THAT'S...
...RIGHT!
ROLL, MOVE YOUR PIECE AND I'LL GIVE YOU ANOTHER QUESTION.
HMMM, THIS ONE'S A LITTLE HARDER. IT'S NOT A MULTIPLE CHOICE.
DESCRIBE LIFE AFTER DEATH.

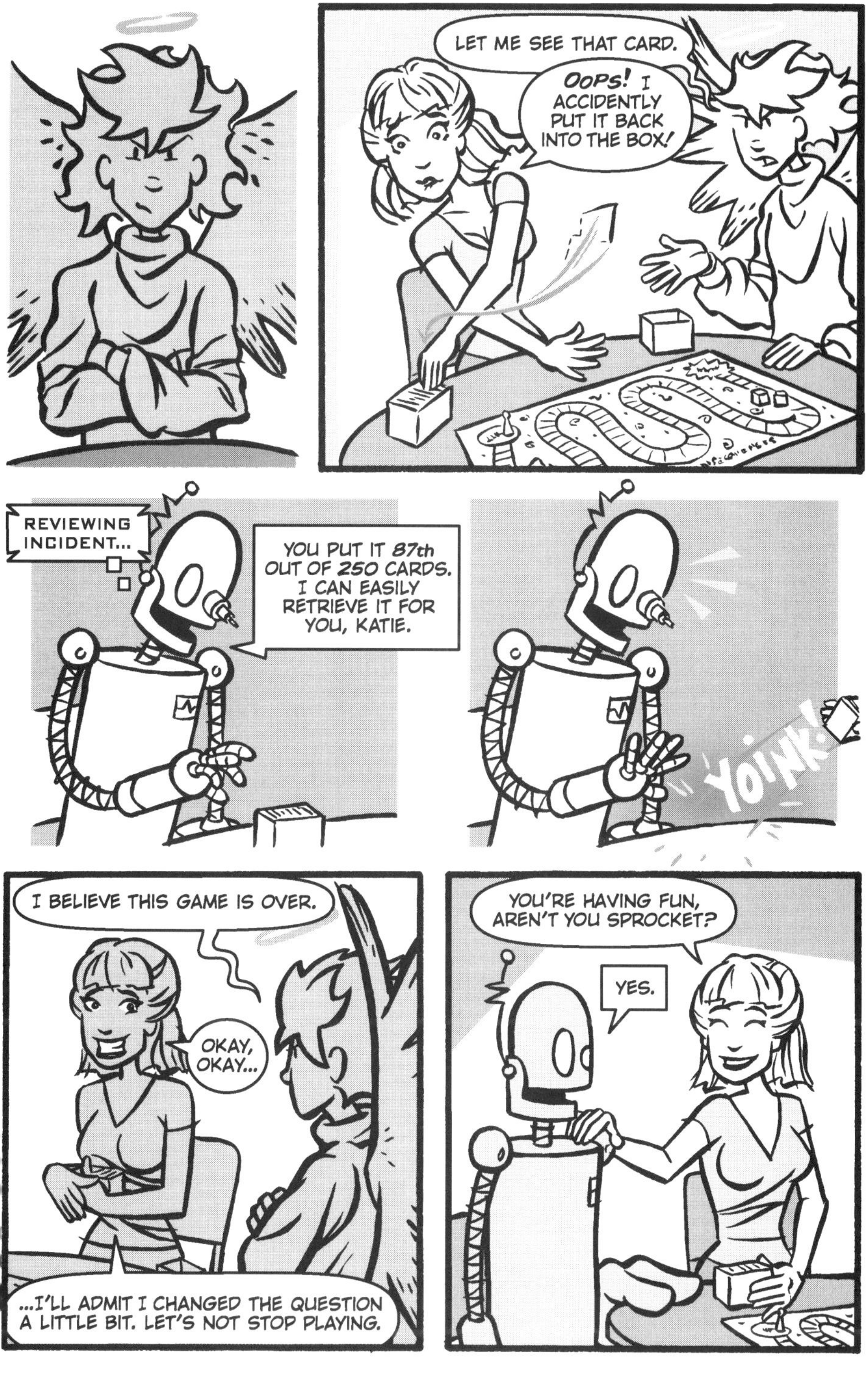
LET ME SEE THAT CARD.
OOPS! I ACCIDENTLY PUT IT BACK INTO THE BOX!
REVIEWING INCIDENT...
YOU PUT IT 87th OUT OF 250 CARDS. I CAN EASILY RETRIEVE IT FOR YOU, KATIE.
YOINK!
I BELIEVE THIS GAME IS OVER.
OKAY, OKAY...
...I'LL ADMIT I CHANGED THE QUESTION A LITTLE BIT. LET'S NOT STOP PLAYING.
YOU'RE HAVING FUN, AREN'T YOU SPROCKET?
YES.

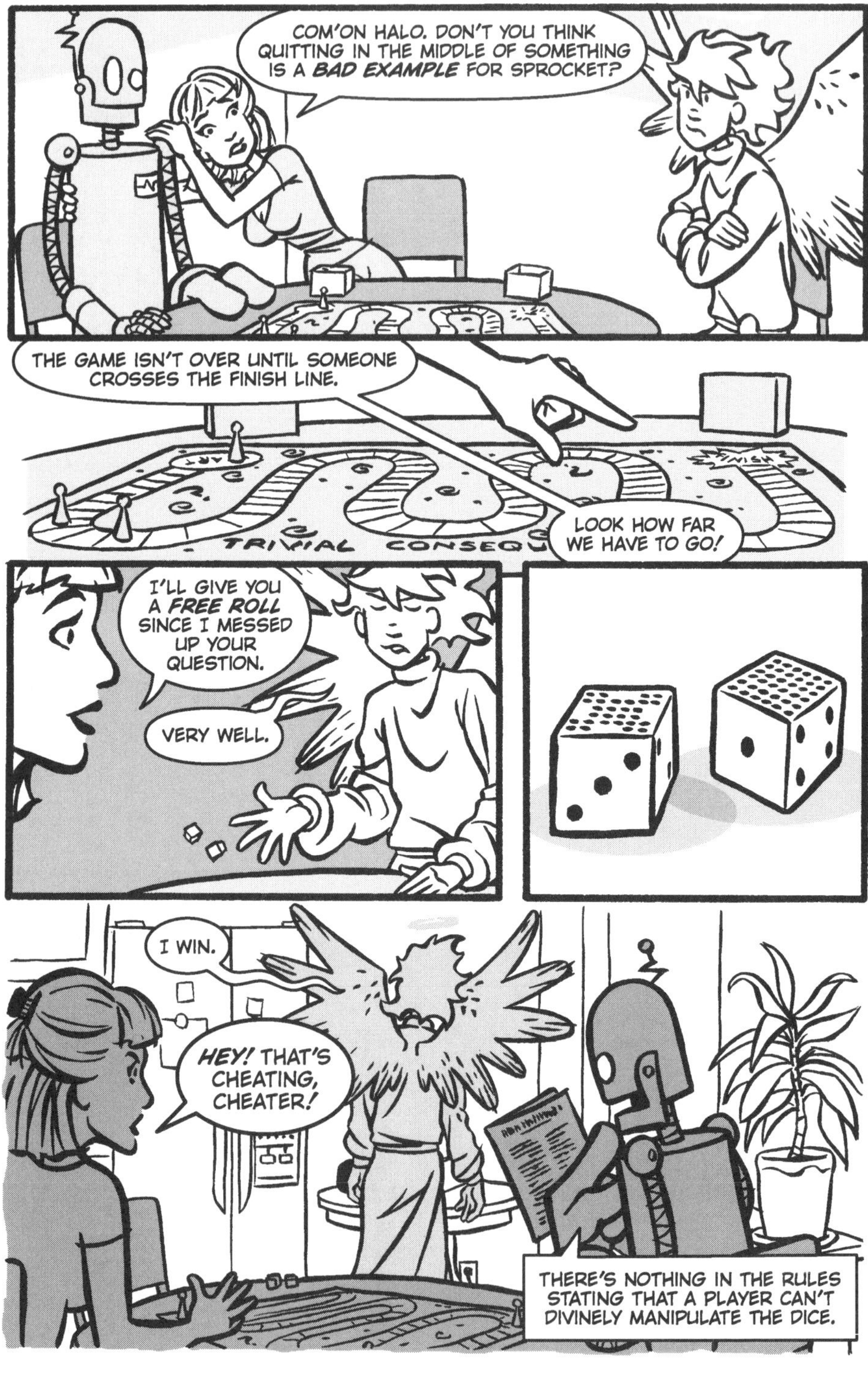
COM'ON HALO. DON'T YOU THINK QUITTING IN THE MIDDLE OF SOMETHING IS A *BAD EXAMPLE* FOR SPROCKET?
THE GAME ISN'T OVER UNTIL SOMEONE CROSSES THE FINISH LINE.
ART
FINISH
TRIVIAL CONSEQU
LOOK HOW FAR WE HAVE TO GO!
I'LL GIVE YOU A *FREE ROLL* SINCE I MESSED UP YOUR QUESTION.
VERY WELL.
I WIN.
HEY! THAT'S CHEATING, CHEATER!
THERE'S NOTHING IN THE RULES STATING THAT A PLAYER CAN'T DIVINELY MANIPULATE THE DICE.

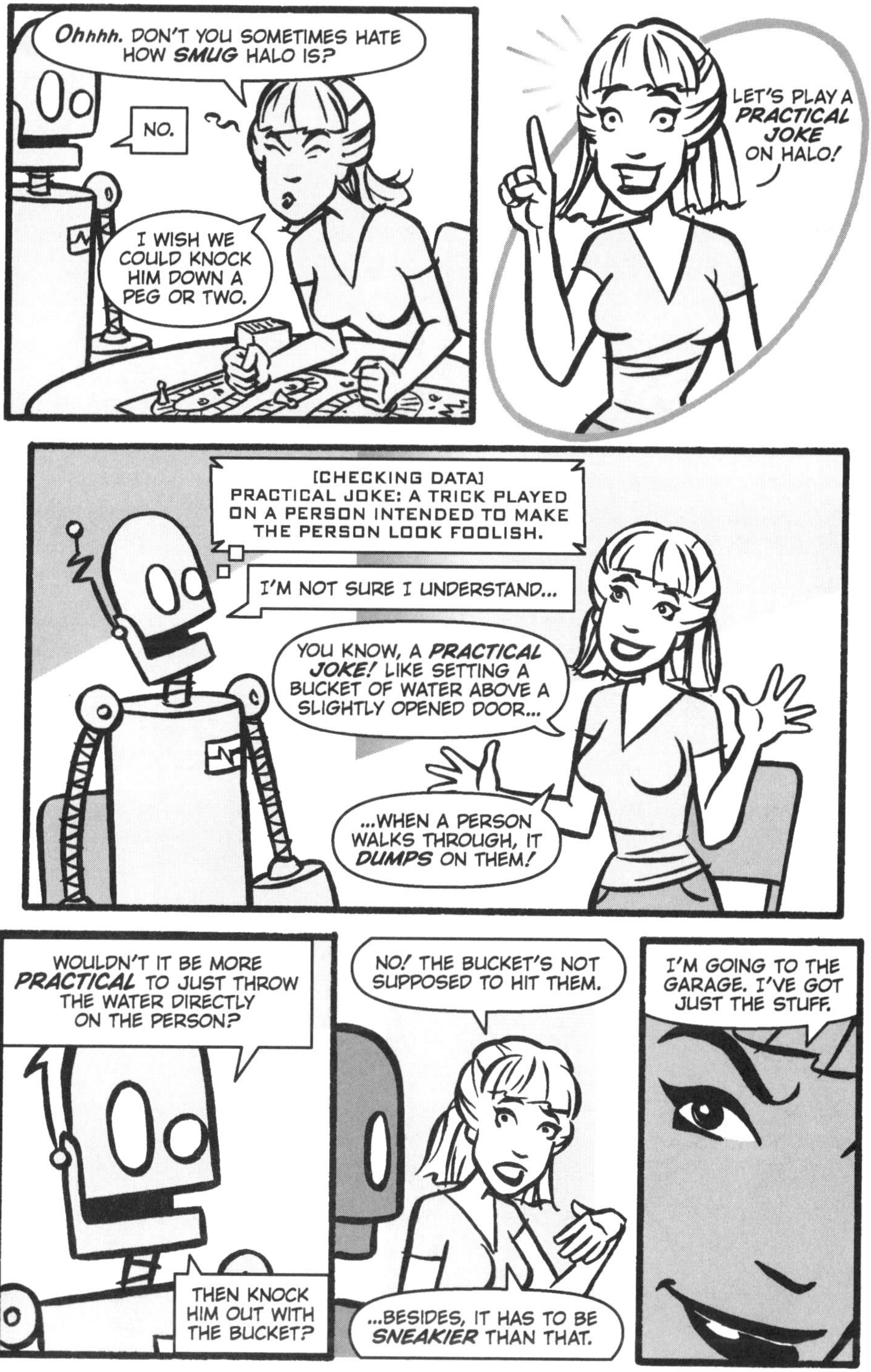
Ohhhh. DON'T YOU SOMETIMES HATE HOW SMUG HALO IS?
NO.
I WISH WE COULD KNOCK HIM DOWN A PEG OR TWO.
LET'S PLAY A PRACTICAL JOKE ON HALO!
[CHECKING DATA] PRACTICAL JOKE: A TRICK PLAYED ON A PERSON INTENDED TO MAKE THE PERSON LOOK FOOLISH.
I'M NOT SURE I UNDERSTAND...
YOU KNOW, A PRACTICAL JOKE! LIKE SETTING A BUCKET OF WATER ABOVE A SLIGHTLY OPENED DOOR...
...WHEN A PERSON WALKS THROUGH, IT DUMPS ON THEM!
WOULDN'T IT BE MORE PRACTICAL TO JUST THROW THE WATER DIRECTLY ON THE PERSON?
THEN KNOCK HIM OUT WITH THE BUCKET?
NO! THE BUCKET'S NOT SUPPOSED TO HIT THEM.
...BESIDES, IT HAS TO BE SNEAKIER THAN THAT.
I'M GOING TO THE GARAGE. I'VE GOT JUST THE STUFF.

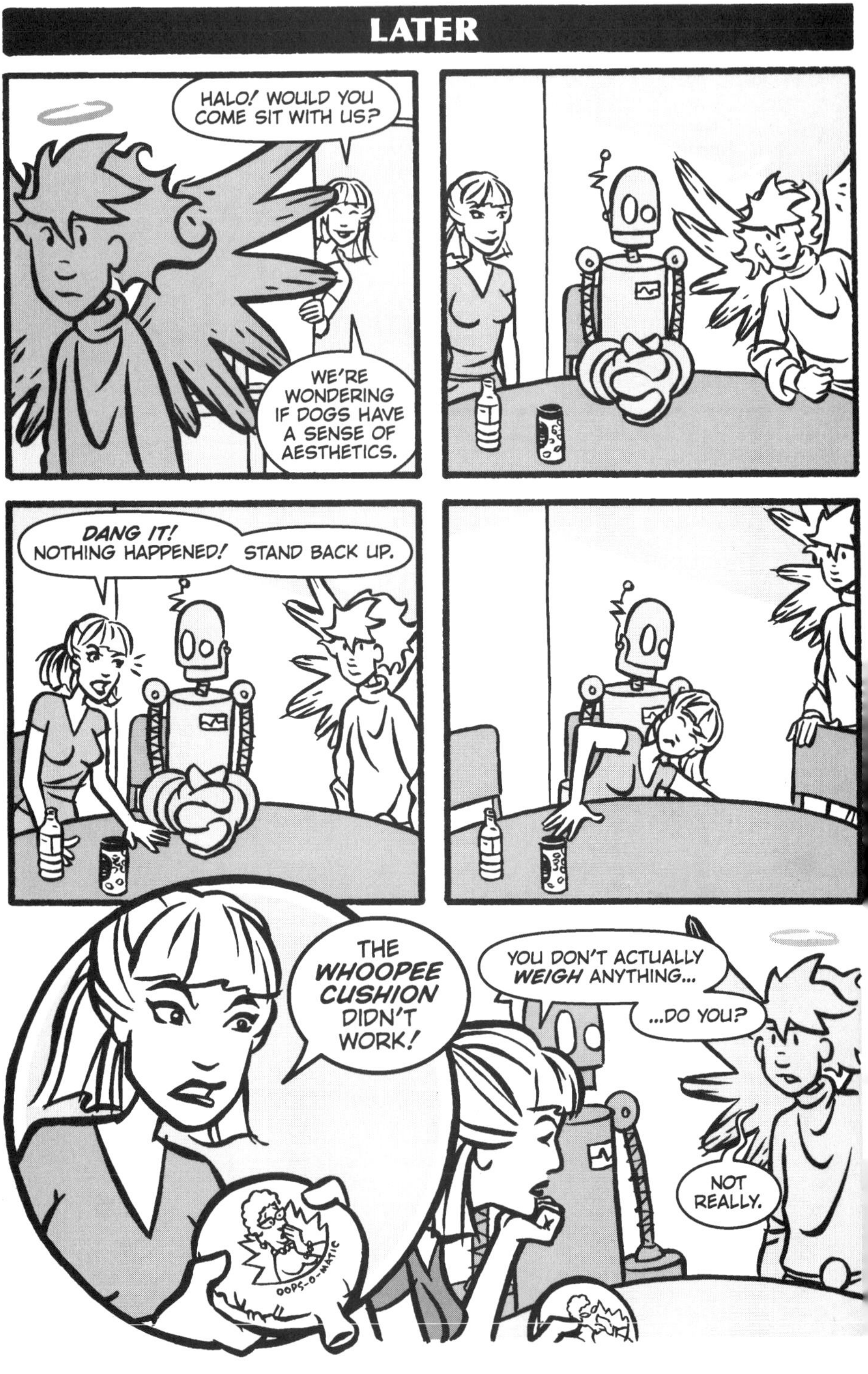
LATER
HALO! WOULD YOU COME SIT WITH US?
WE'RE WONDERING IF DOGS HAVE A SENSE OF AESTHETICS.
DANG IT! NOTHING HAPPENED!
STAND BACK UP.
THE WHOOPEE CUSHION DIDN'T WORK!
YOU DON'T ACTUALLY WEIGH ANYTHING...
...DO YOU?
NOT REALLY.
OOPS-O-MATIC

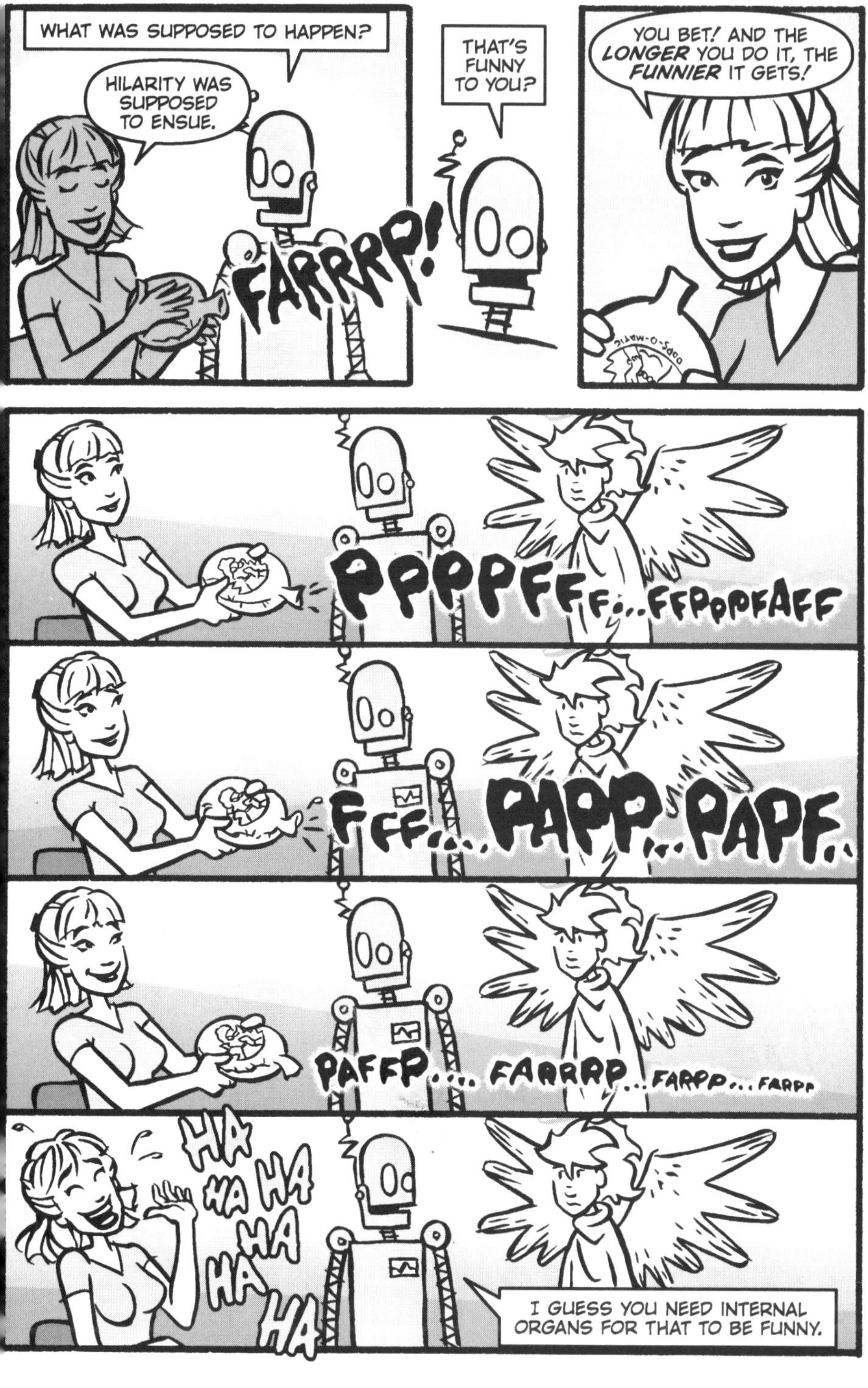
WHAT WAS SUPPOSED TO HAPPEN?
HILARITY WAS SUPPOSED TO ENSUE.
FARRRP!
THAT'S FUNNY TO YOU?
YOU BET! AND THE *LONGER* YOU DO IT, THE *FUNNIER* IT GETS!
PPPPFFFF...FFPPPFAFF
FFF... PAPP... PAPF..
PAFFP.... FARRRP...FARPP...FARPP
HA HA HA HA HA HA HA
I GUESS YOU NEED INTERNAL ORGANS FOR THAT TO BE FUNNY.

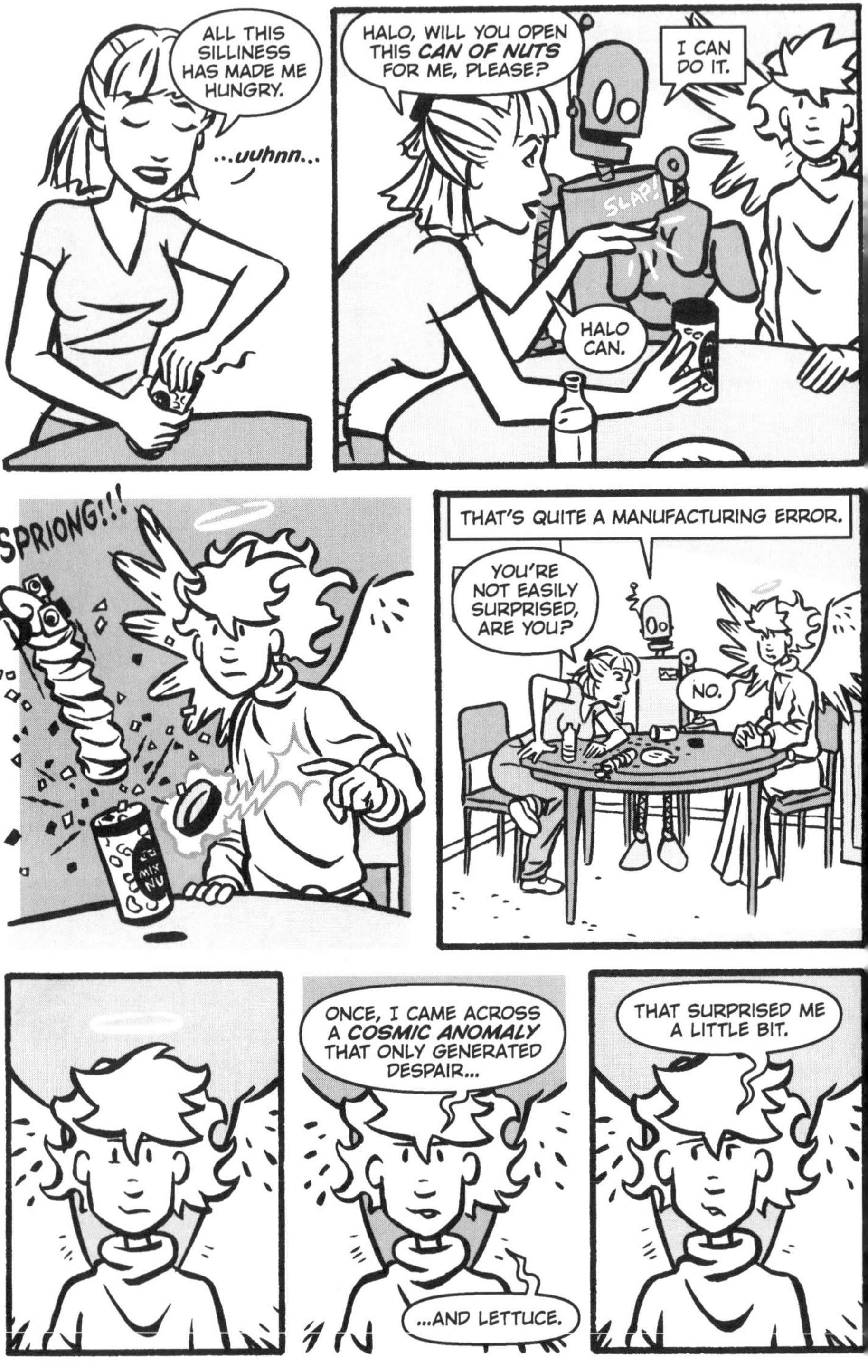
ALL THIS SILLINESS HAS MADE ME HUNGRY.
...uuhnn...
HALO, WILL YOU OPEN THIS CAN OF NUTS FOR ME, PLEASE?
I CAN DO IT.
SLAP!
HALO CAN.
SPRIONG!!!
THAT'S QUITE A MANUFACTURING ERROR.
YOU'RE NOT EASILY SURPRISED, ARE YOU?
NO.
ONCE, I CAME ACROSS A COSMIC ANOMALY THAT ONLY GENERATED DESPAIR...
...AND LETTUCE.
THAT SURPRISED ME A LITTLE BIT.

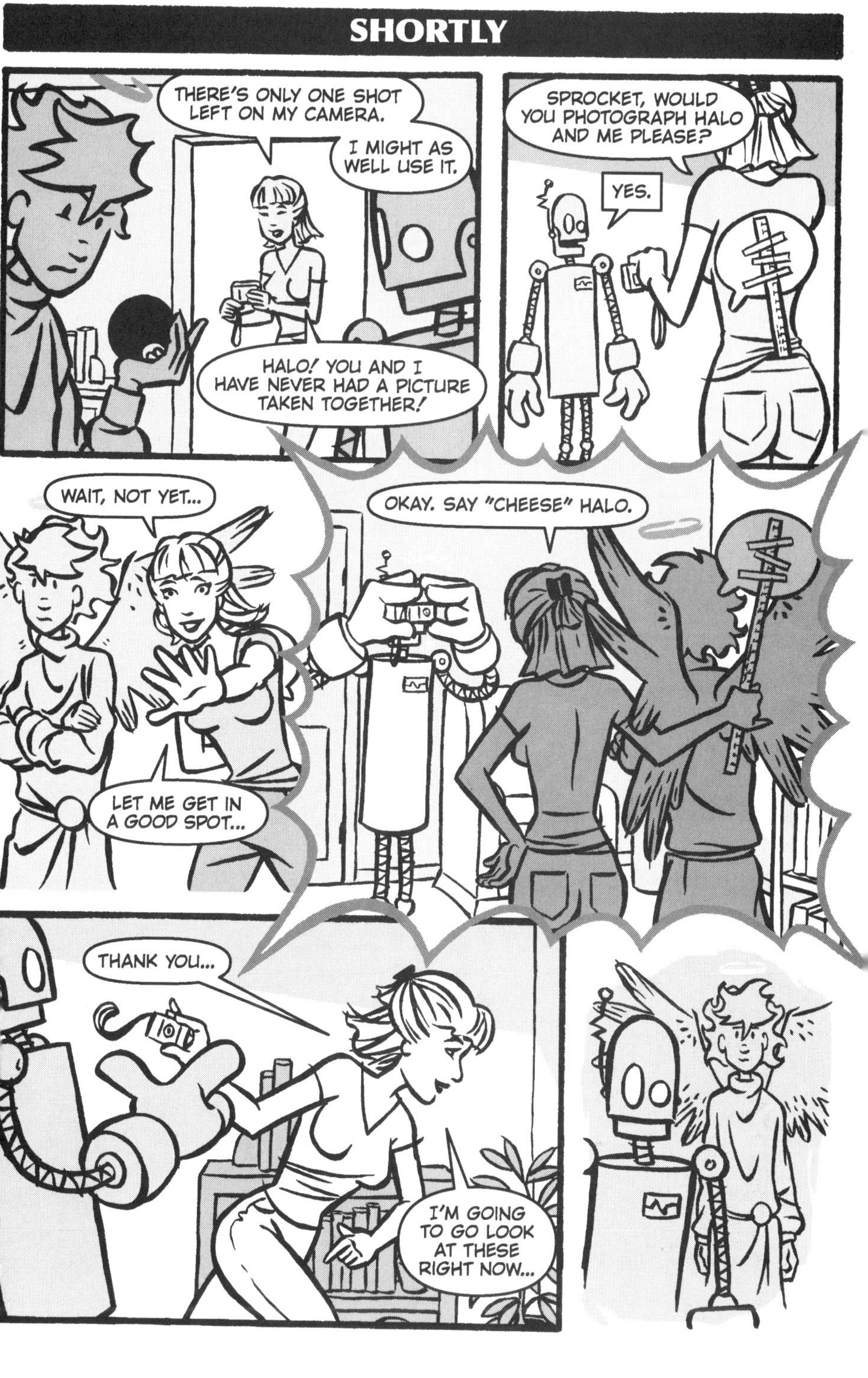
SHORTLY
THERE'S ONLY ONE SHOT LEFT ON MY CAMERA.
I MIGHT AS WELL USE IT.
HALO! YOU AND I HAVE NEVER HAD A PICTURE TAKEN TOGETHER!
SPROCKET, WOULD YOU PHOTOGRAPH HALO AND ME PLEASE?
YES.
WAIT, NOT YET...
LET ME GET IN A GOOD SPOT...
OKAY. SAY "CHEESE" HALO.
THANK YOU...
I'M GOING TO GO LOOK AT THESE RIGHT NOW...

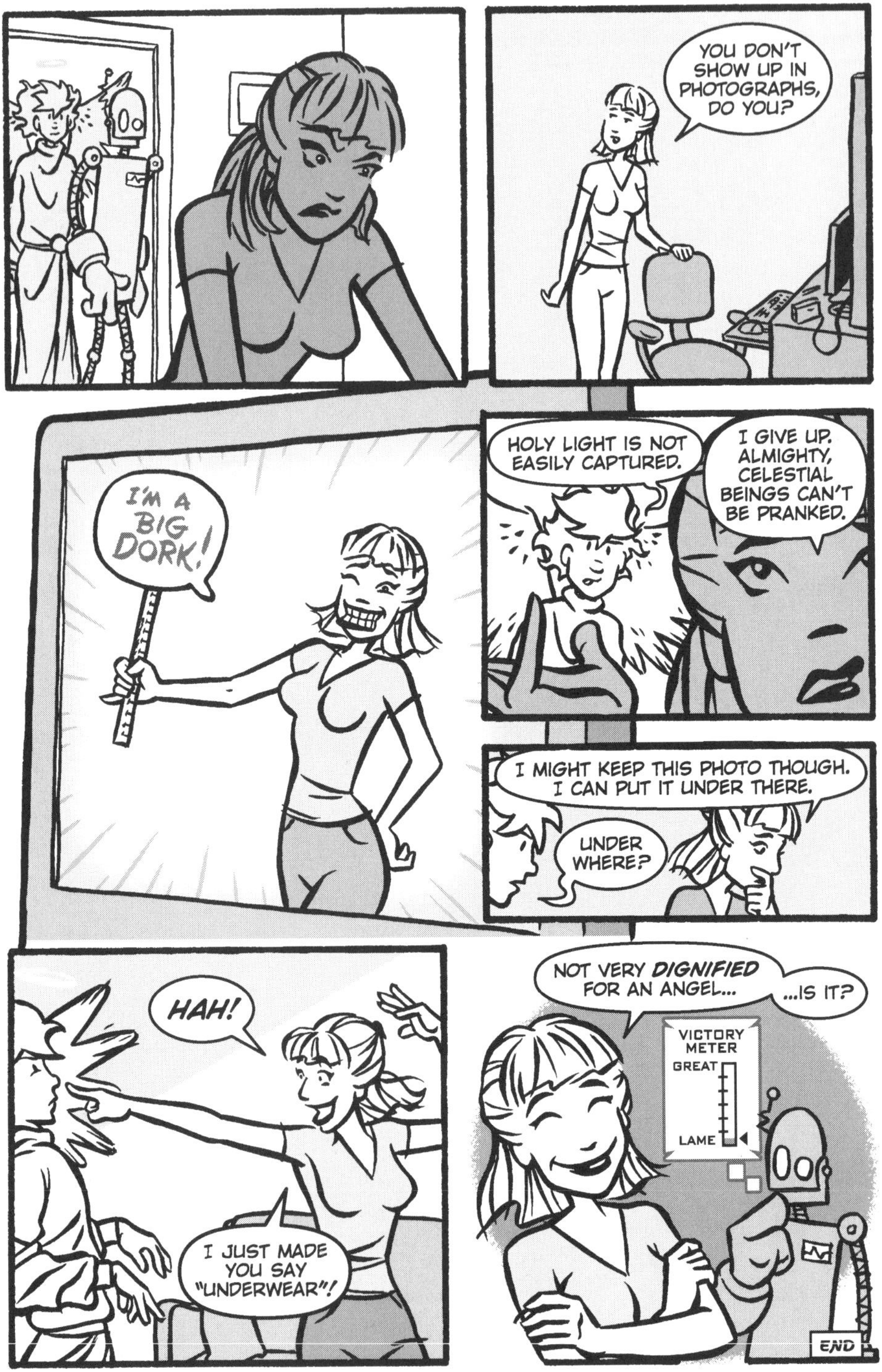
YOU DON'T SHOW UP IN PHOTOGRAPHS, DO YOU?
I'M A BIG DORK!
HOLY LIGHT IS NOT EASILY CAPTURED.
I GIVE UP. ALMIGHTY, CELESTIAL BEINGS CAN'T BE PRANKED.
I MIGHT KEEP THIS PHOTO THOUGH. I CAN PUT IT UNDER THERE.
UNDER WHERE?
HAH!
I JUST MADE YOU SAY "UNDERWEAR"!
NOT VERY *DIGNIFIED* FOR AN ANGEL...
...IS IT?
VICTORY METER
GREAT
LAME
END

HALO AND SPROCKET

"SIT FOR A SPELL"

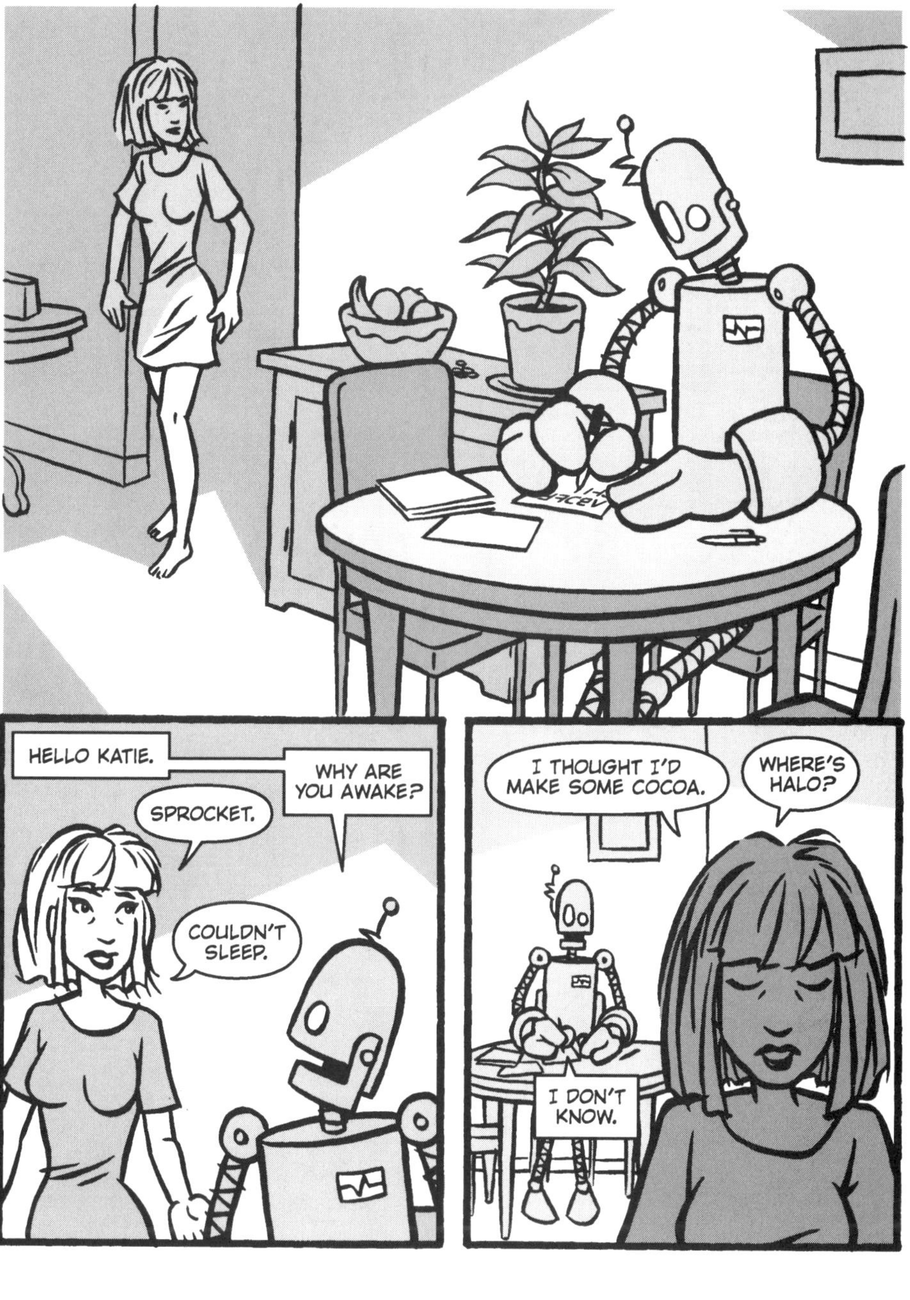
HELLO KATIE.
SPROCKET.
WHY ARE YOU AWAKE?
COULDN'T SLEEP.
I THOUGHT I'D MAKE SOME COCOA.
WHERE'S HALO?
I DON'T KNOW.

WHAT ARE YOU DOING?

FIXING THE ALPHABET.

REALLY.

YES. IT'S NOT VERY EFFICIENT.

IT DOESN'T NEED A **C**. IT MAKES THE SAME SOUND AS A **K** OR AN **S**.

(YOU WILL HAVE TO RESPELL SOME WORDS OF COURSE.)

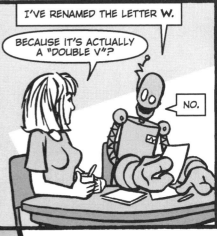

I'VE RENAMED THE LETTER **W**.

BECAUSE IT'S ACTUALLY A "DOUBLE V"?

NO.

ALL THE OTHER LETTERS ARE PRONOUNCED WITH A SINGLE SYLLABLE, BUT **W** HAS THREE!

PLUS, EVERY LETTER HAS ITS OWN SOUND IN ITS NAME. **A** HAS AN "A" SOUND. **B** HAS A "B" SOUND. **D** HAS A "D" SOUND...

I GET IT.

I WOULD LIKE TO RENAMED **W** "WO".

Y SHOULD BE RENAMED "YI" TO REFLECT BOTH ITS CONSONANT AND VOWEL SOUND.

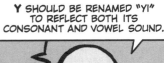

...THOUGH IT WOULD BE BETTER TO NEVER USE IT AS A VOWEL.

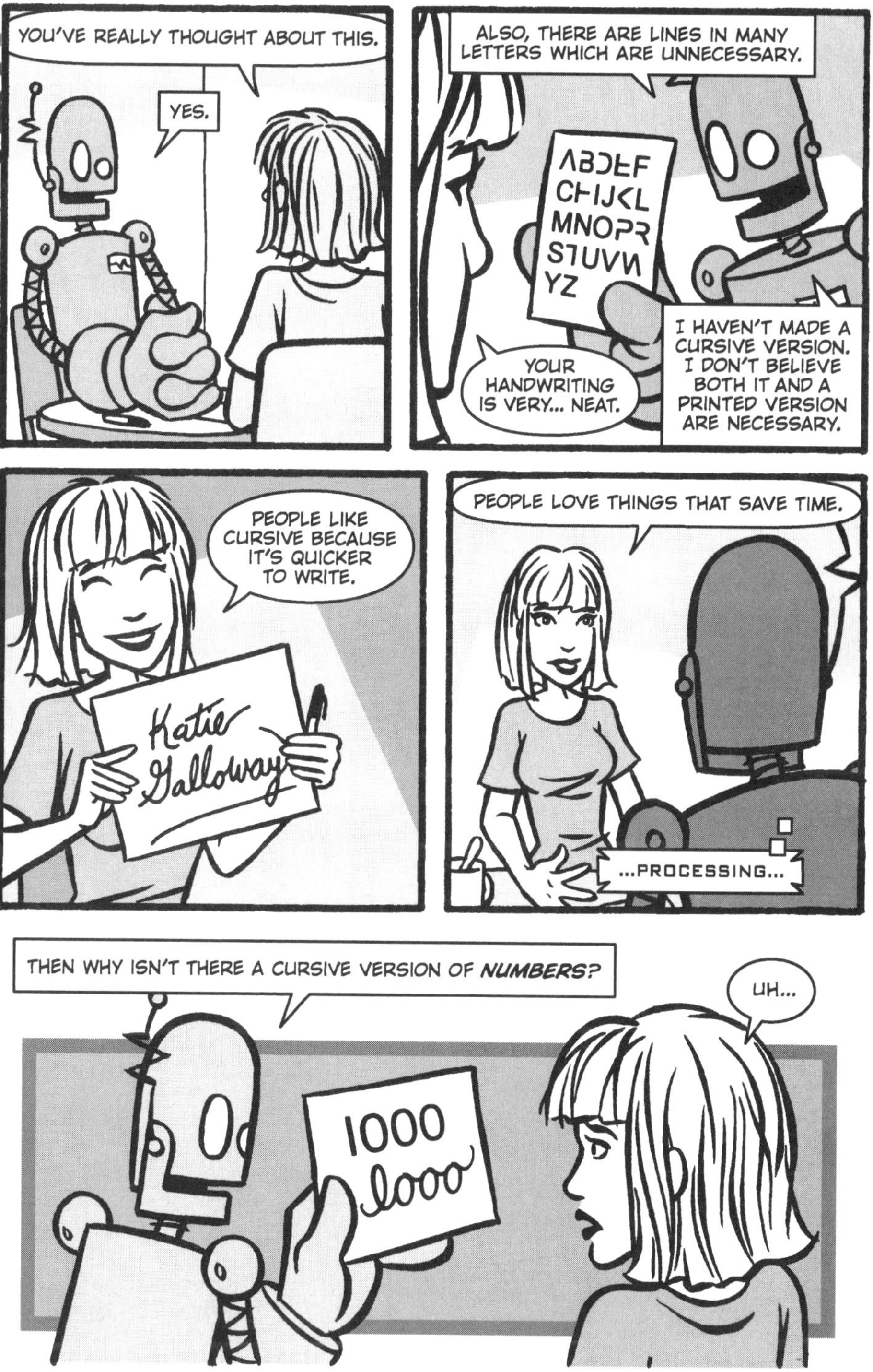
YOU'VE REALLY THOUGHT ABOUT THIS.
YES.
ALSO, THERE ARE LINES IN MANY LETTERS WHICH ARE UNNECESSARY.
ABDEF CHIJKL MNOPR STUVW YZ
YOUR HANDWRITING IS VERY... NEAT.
I HAVEN'T MADE A CURSIVE VERSION. I DON'T BELIEVE BOTH IT AND A PRINTED VERSION ARE NECESSARY.
PEOPLE LIKE CURSIVE BECAUSE IT'S QUICKER TO WRITE.
Katie Galloway
PEOPLE LOVE THINGS THAT SAVE TIME.
...PROCESSING...
THEN WHY ISN'T THERE A CURSIVE VERSION OF *NUMBERS*?
1000
1000
UH...

YOU MAY HAVE NOTICED I'VE ALSO LEFT **Q** AND **X** OUT OF MY NEW ALPHABET.

THE **Q** SOUND IS MERELY A **KW** SOUND.

X ESSENTIALLY FUNCTIONS THE SAME AS A **Z** OR A **KS** COMBINATION.

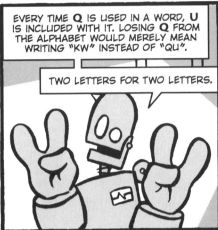

EVERY TIME **Q** IS USED IN A WORD, **U** IS INCLUDED WITH IT. LOSING **Q** FROM THE ALPHABET WOULD MERELY MEAN WRITING "KW" INSTEAD OF "QU".

TWO LETTERS FOR TWO LETTERS.

BUT IT TAKES LONGER TO WRITE "KS" THAN "X".

I DON'T KNOW IF IT'S BETTER TO HAVE AN EFFICIENT ALPHABET, OR A SHORTER WRITING TIME FOR WORDS WITH **X** IN THEM.

IT'S QUITE A DILEMMA.

TAP TAP

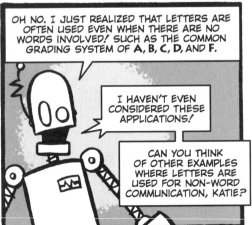

OH NO. I JUST REALIZED THAT LETTERS ARE OFTEN USED EVEN WHEN THERE ARE NO WORDS INVOLVED! SUCH AS THE COMMON GRADING SYSTEM OF **A, B, C, D,** AND **F**.

I HAVEN'T EVEN CONSIDERED THESE APPLICATIONS!

CAN YOU THINK OF OTHER EXAMPLES WHERE LETTERS ARE USED FOR NON-WORD COMMUNICATION, KATIE?

zZZzzZzzz

END

HALO AND SPROCKET BONUS MATERIAL

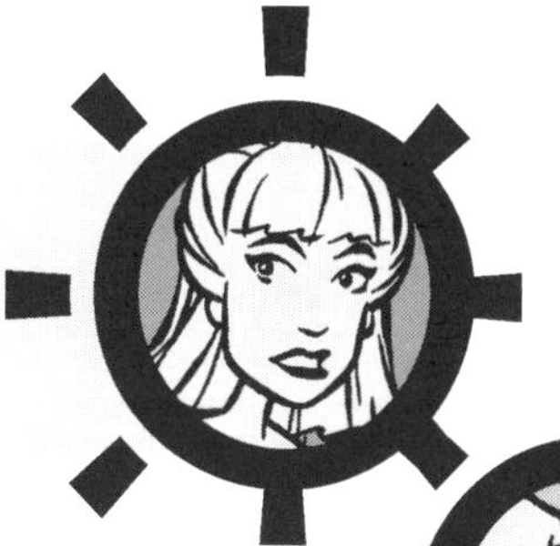

Newspaper Strips

Presenting four strips that originally ran in the Kansas City Star.

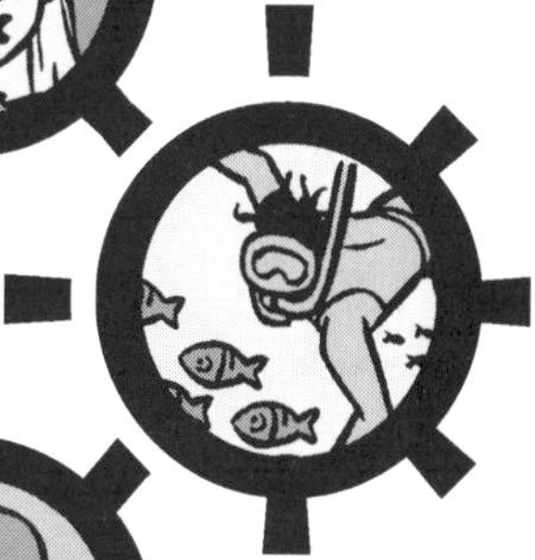

Puzzle Page

Stimulate your brain.
(Not really.)

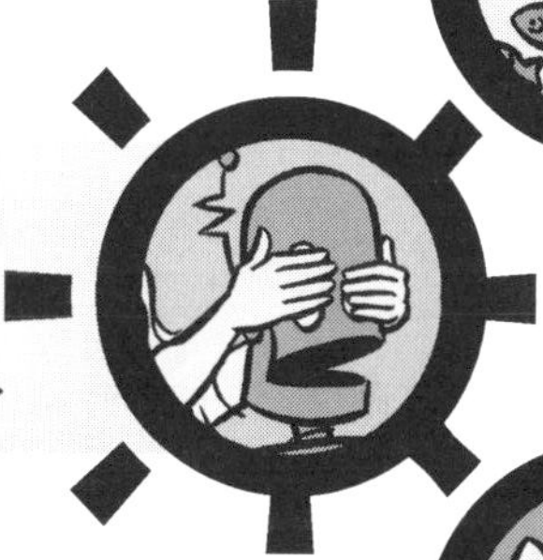

Head Games

First appeared in a program book for STAPLE!, the Independent Media Expo.

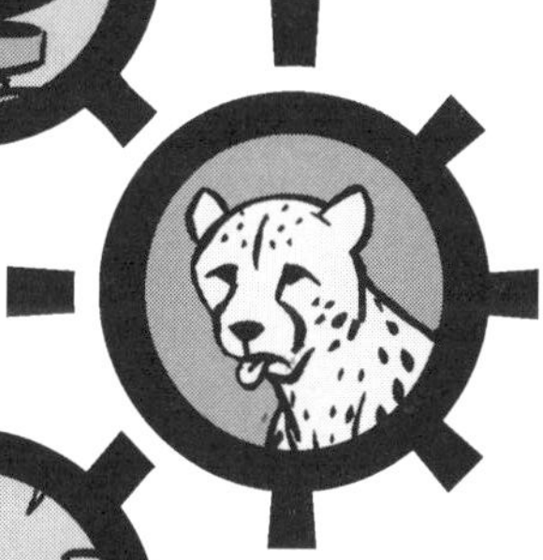

Big Cat Puns

Yep.

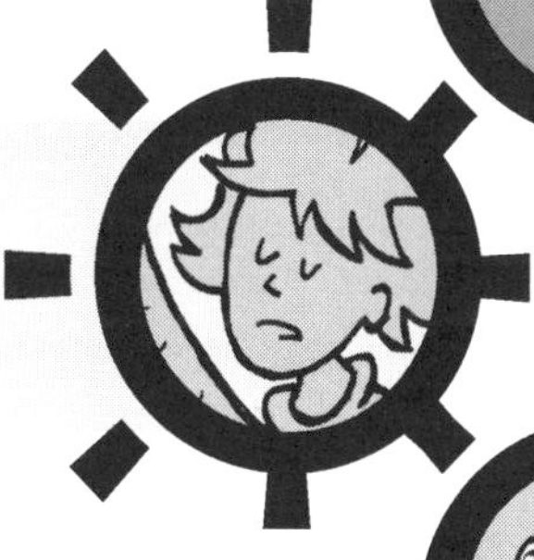

Guest Strip

by Bob Lipski

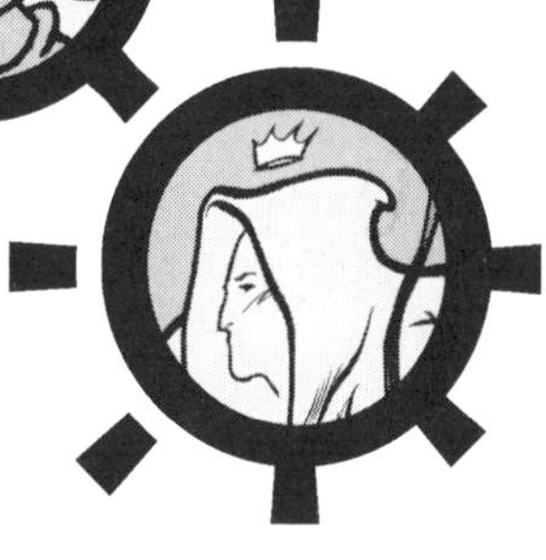

Gallery

Paige Braddock!
Mike Huddleston!
Freddie Williams II!
Kerry Callen!

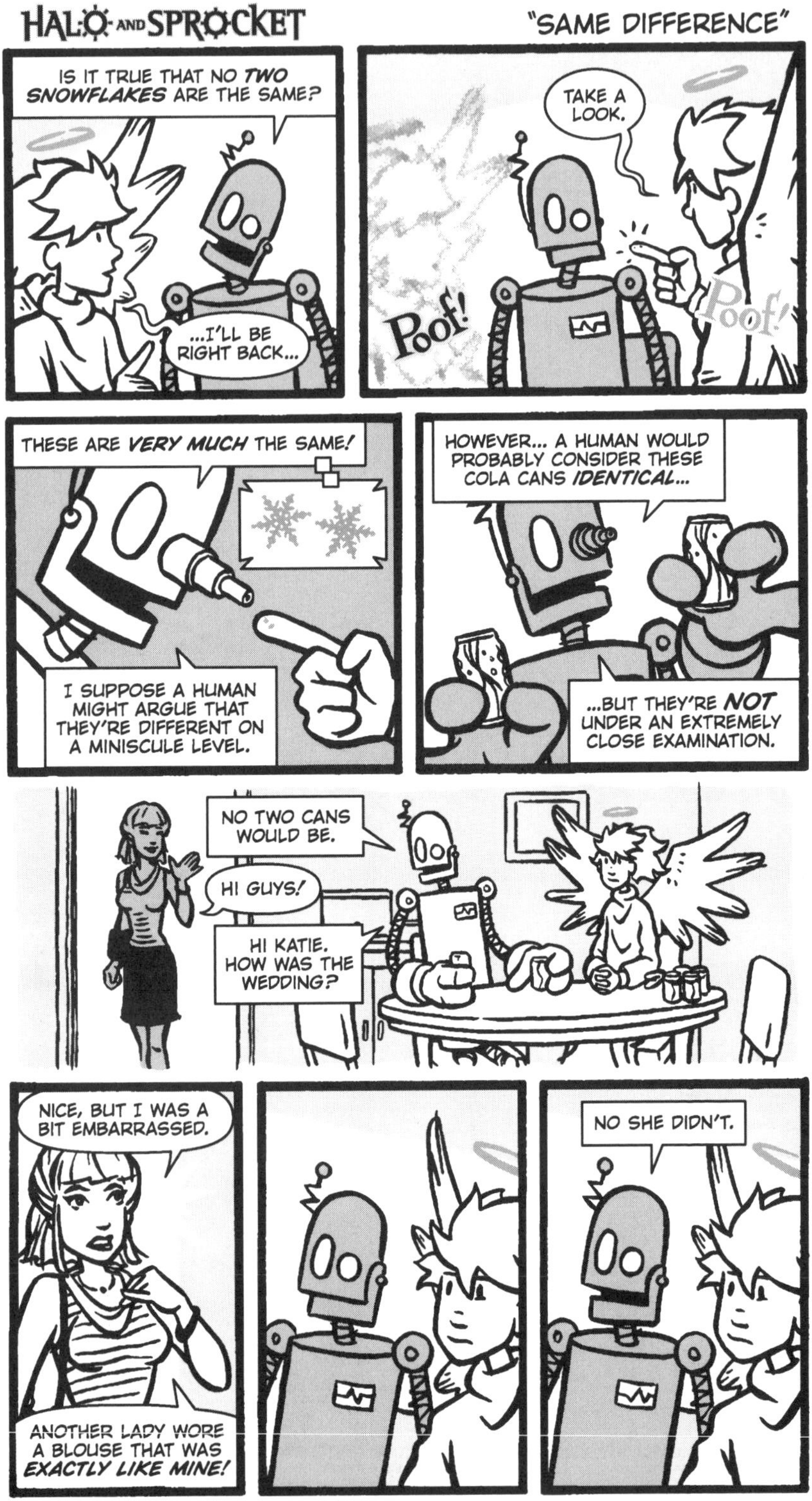
HALO AND SPROCKET
"SAME DIFFERENCE"
IS IT TRUE THAT NO TWO SNOWFLAKES ARE THE SAME?
...I'LL BE RIGHT BACK...
TAKE A LOOK.
Poof!
Poof!
THESE ARE VERY MUCH THE SAME!
I SUPPOSE A HUMAN MIGHT ARGUE THAT THEY'RE DIFFERENT ON A MINISCULE LEVEL.
HOWEVER... A HUMAN WOULD PROBABLY CONSIDER THESE COLA CANS IDENTICAL...
...BUT THEY'RE NOT UNDER AN EXTREMELY CLOSE EXAMINATION.
NO TWO CANS WOULD BE.
HI GUYS!
HI KATIE. HOW WAS THE WEDDING?
NICE, BUT I WAS A BIT EMBARRASSED.
ANOTHER LADY WORE A BLOUSE THAT WAS EXACTLY LIKE MINE!
NO SHE DIDN'T.

HALO AND SPROCKET

"FACE IT"

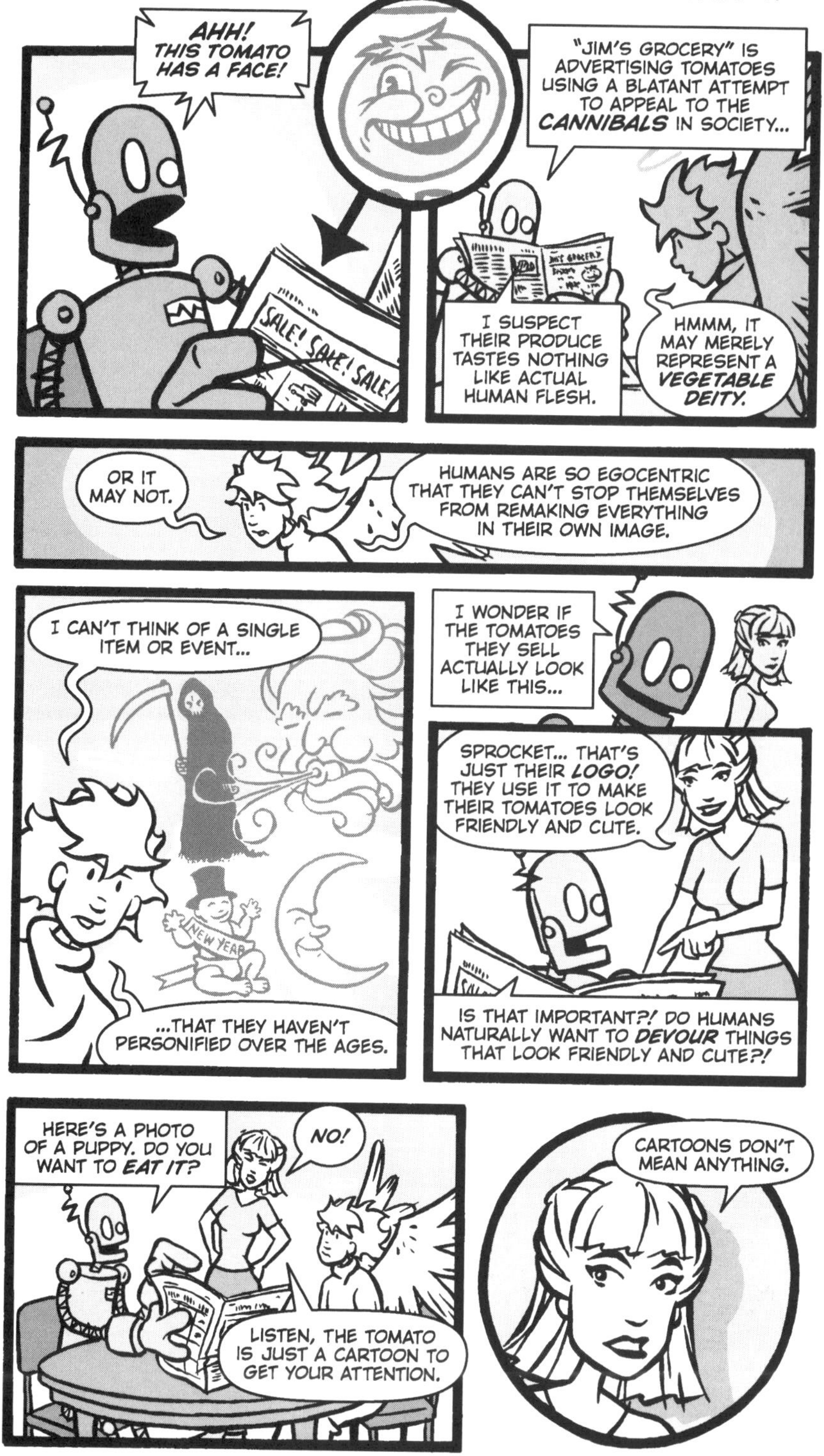
AHH! THIS TOMATO HAS A FACE!
SALE! SALE! SALE!
"JIM'S GROCERY" IS ADVERTISING TOMATOES USING A BLATANT ATTEMPT TO APPEAL TO THE CANNIBALS IN SOCIETY...
I SUSPECT THEIR PRODUCE TASTES NOTHING LIKE ACTUAL HUMAN FLESH.
HMMM, IT MAY MERELY REPRESENT A VEGETABLE DEITY.
OR IT MAY NOT.
HUMANS ARE SO EGOCENTRIC THAT THEY CAN'T STOP THEMSELVES FROM REMAKING EVERYTHING IN THEIR OWN IMAGE.
I CAN'T THINK OF A SINGLE ITEM OR EVENT...
NEW YEAR
...THAT THEY HAVEN'T PERSONIFIED OVER THE AGES.
I WONDER IF THE TOMATOES THEY SELL ACTUALLY LOOK LIKE THIS...
SPROCKET... THAT'S JUST THEIR LOGO! THEY USE IT TO MAKE THEIR TOMATOES LOOK FRIENDLY AND CUTE.
IS THAT IMPORTANT?! DO HUMANS NATURALLY WANT TO DEVOUR THINGS THAT LOOK FRIENDLY AND CUTE?!
HERE'S A PHOTO OF A PUPPY. DO YOU WANT TO EAT IT?
NO!
LISTEN, THE TOMATO IS JUST A CARTOON TO GET YOUR ATTENTION.
CARTOONS DON'T MEAN ANYTHING.

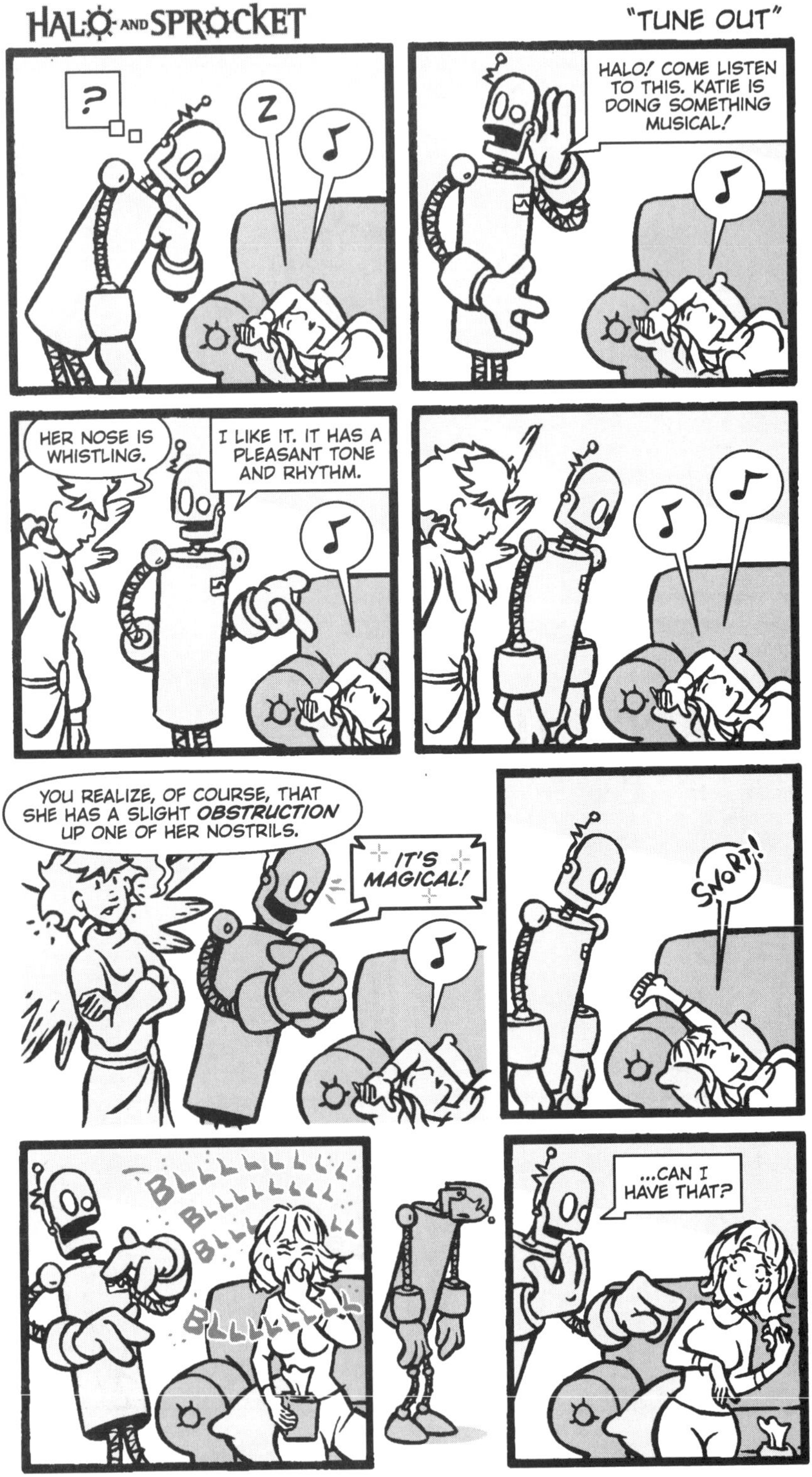
HALO AND SPROCKET
"TUNE OUT"
?
Z
HALO! COME LISTEN TO THIS. KATIE IS DOING SOMETHING MUSICAL!
HER NOSE IS WHISTLING.
I LIKE IT. IT HAS A PLEASANT TONE AND RHYTHM.
YOU REALIZE, OF COURSE, THAT SHE HAS A SLIGHT OBSTRUCTION UP ONE OF HER NOSTRILS.
IT'S MAGICAL!
SNORT!
BLLLLLLLLL
BLLLLLLLL
BLLL
BLLLLLLLL
...CAN I HAVE THAT?

HALO AND SPROCKET

"WATCH THIS"

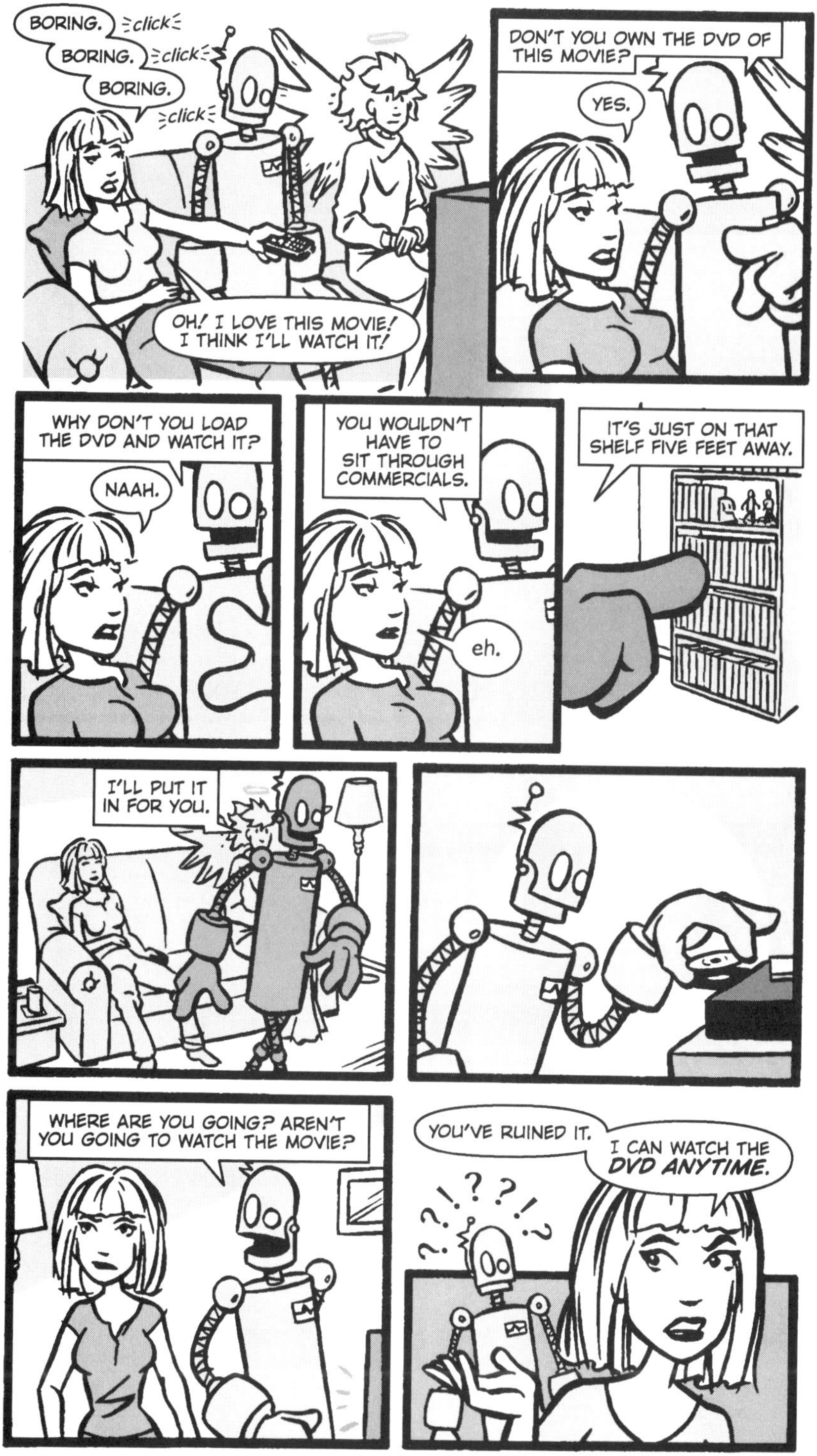
BORING.
click
BORING.
click
BORING.
click
OH! I LOVE THIS MOVIE! I THINK I'LL WATCH IT!
DON'T YOU OWN THE DVD OF THIS MOVIE?
YES.
WHY DON'T YOU LOAD THE DVD AND WATCH IT?
NAAH.
YOU WOULDN'T HAVE TO SIT THROUGH COMMERCIALS.
eh.
IT'S JUST ON THAT SHELF FIVE FEET AWAY.
I'LL PUT IT IN FOR YOU.
WHERE ARE YOU GOING? AREN'T YOU GOING TO WATCH THE MOVIE?
YOU'VE RUINED IT.
I CAN WATCH THE DVD ANYTIME.
?!?!?!?

HALO and SPROCKET PUZZLE PAGE!

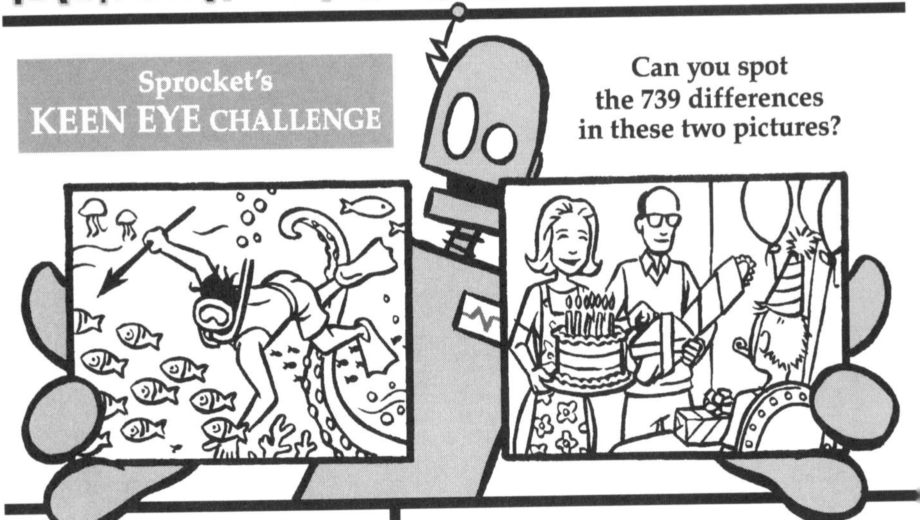

Sprocket's KEEN EYE CHALLENGE
Can you spot the 739 differences in these two pictures?

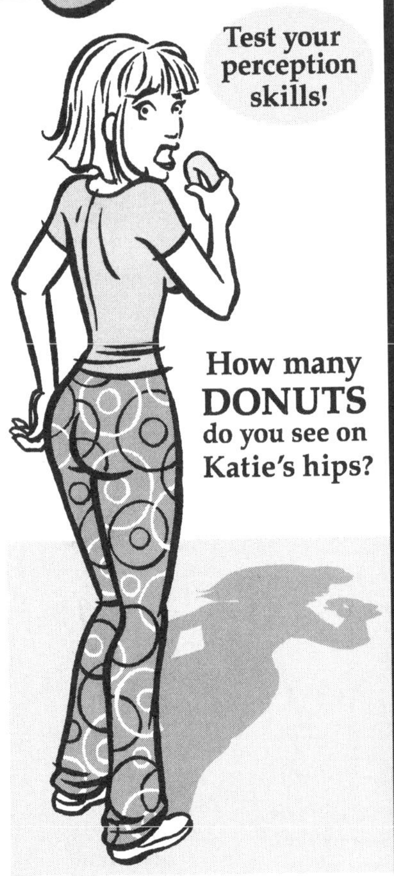

Test your perception skills!
How many DONUTS do you see on Katie's hips?

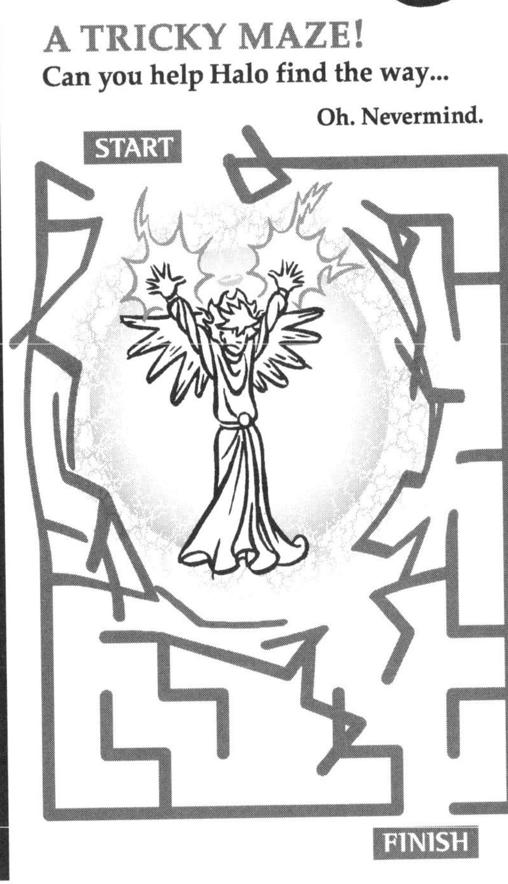

A TRICKY MAZE!
Can you help Halo find the way...
Oh. Nevermind.
START
FINISH

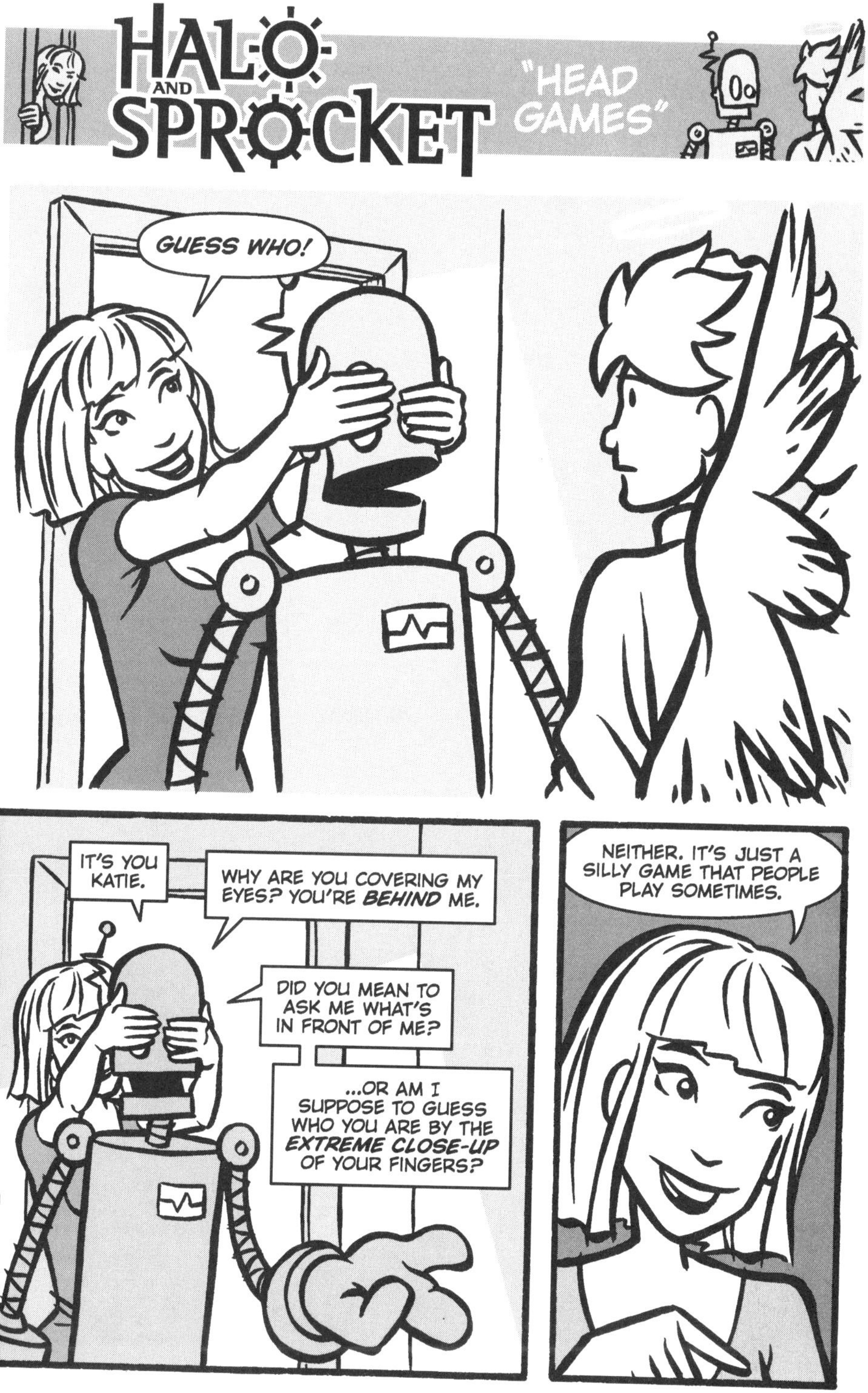
HALO AND SPROCKET
"HEAD GAMES"
GUESS WHO!
IT'S YOU KATIE.
WHY ARE YOU COVERING MY EYES? YOU'RE BEHIND ME.
DID YOU MEAN TO ASK ME WHAT'S IN FRONT OF ME?
...OR AM I SUPPOSE TO GUESS WHO YOU ARE BY THE EXTREME CLOSE-UP OF YOUR FINGERS?
NEITHER. IT'S JUST A SILLY GAME THAT PEOPLE PLAY SOMETIMES.

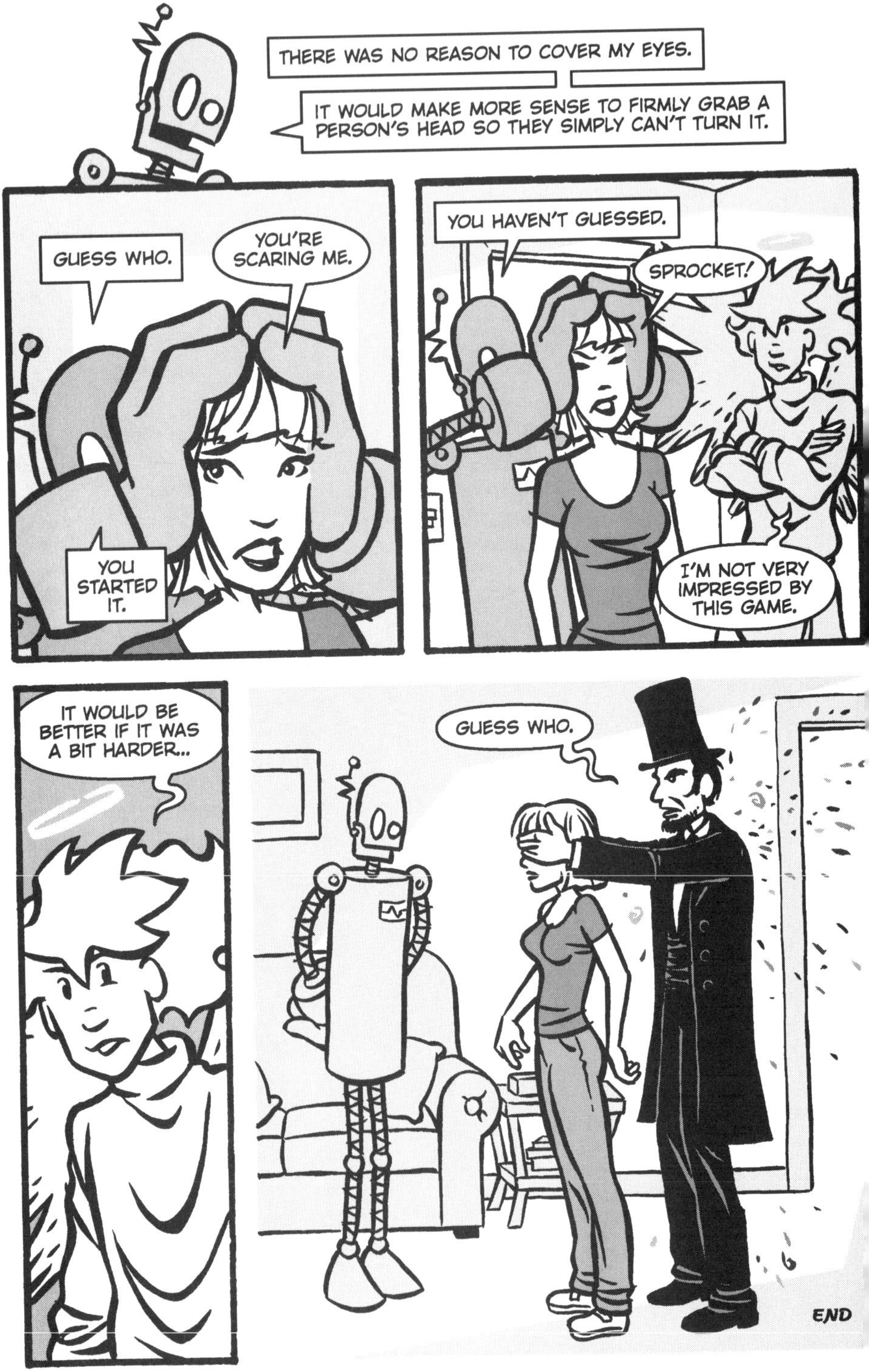
THERE WAS NO REASON TO COVER MY EYES.
IT WOULD MAKE MORE SENSE TO FIRMLY GRAB A PERSON'S HEAD SO THEY SIMPLY CAN'T TURN IT.
GUESS WHO.
YOU'RE SCARING ME.
YOU STARTED IT.
YOU HAVEN'T GUESSED.
SPROCKET!
I'M NOT VERY IMPRESSED BY THIS GAME.
IT WOULD BE BETTER IF IT WAS A BIT HARDER...
GUESS WHO.
END

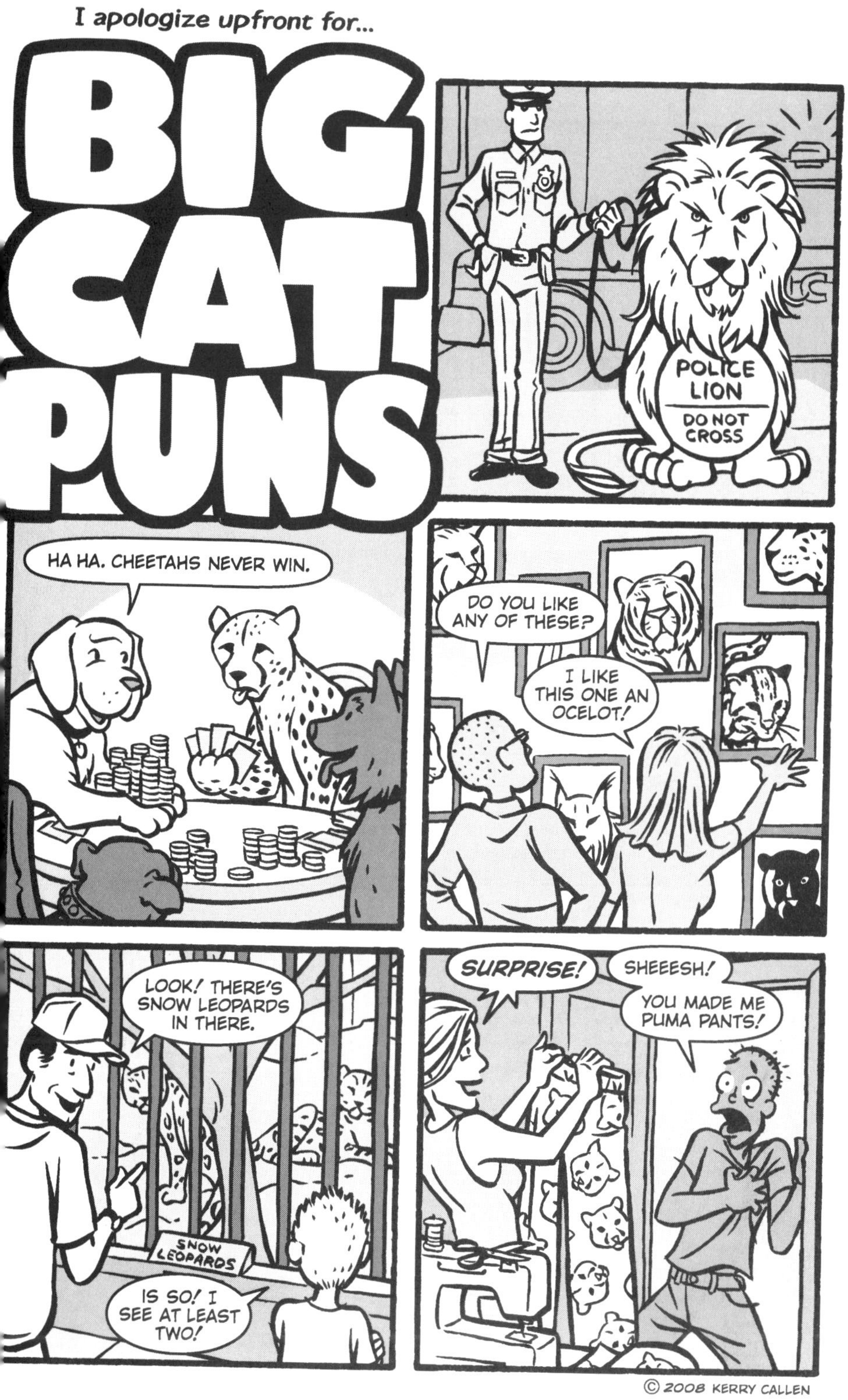
I apologize upfront for...
BIG CAT PUNS
POLICE LION
DO NOT CROSS
HA HA. CHEETAHS NEVER WIN.
DO YOU LIKE ANY OF THESE?
I LIKE THIS ONE AN OCELOT!
LOOK! THERE'S SNOW LEOPARDS IN THERE.
SNOW LEOPARDS
IS SO! I SEE AT LEAST TWO!
SURPRISE!
SHEEESH!
YOU MADE ME PUMA PANTS!

Guest HALO AND SPROCKET Strip by Bob Lipski

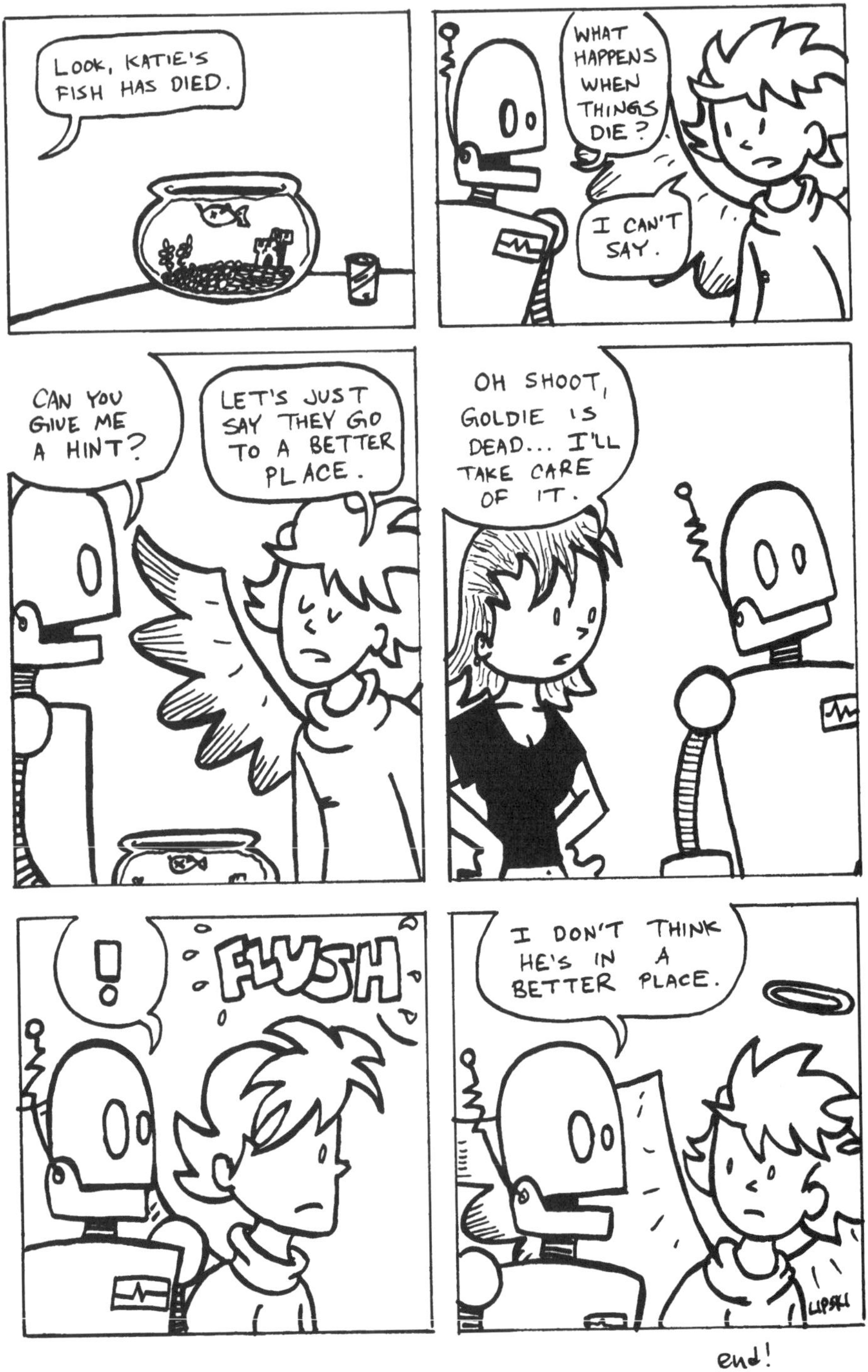
LOOK, KATIE'S FISH HAS DIED.
WHAT HAPPENS WHEN THINGS DIE?
I CAN'T SAY.
CAN YOU GIVE ME A HINT?
LET'S JUST SAY THEY GO TO A BETTER PLACE.
OH SHOOT, GOLDIE IS DEAD... I'LL TAKE CARE OF IT.
!
FLUSH
I DON'T THINK HE'S IN A BETTER PLACE.
LIPSKI

end!

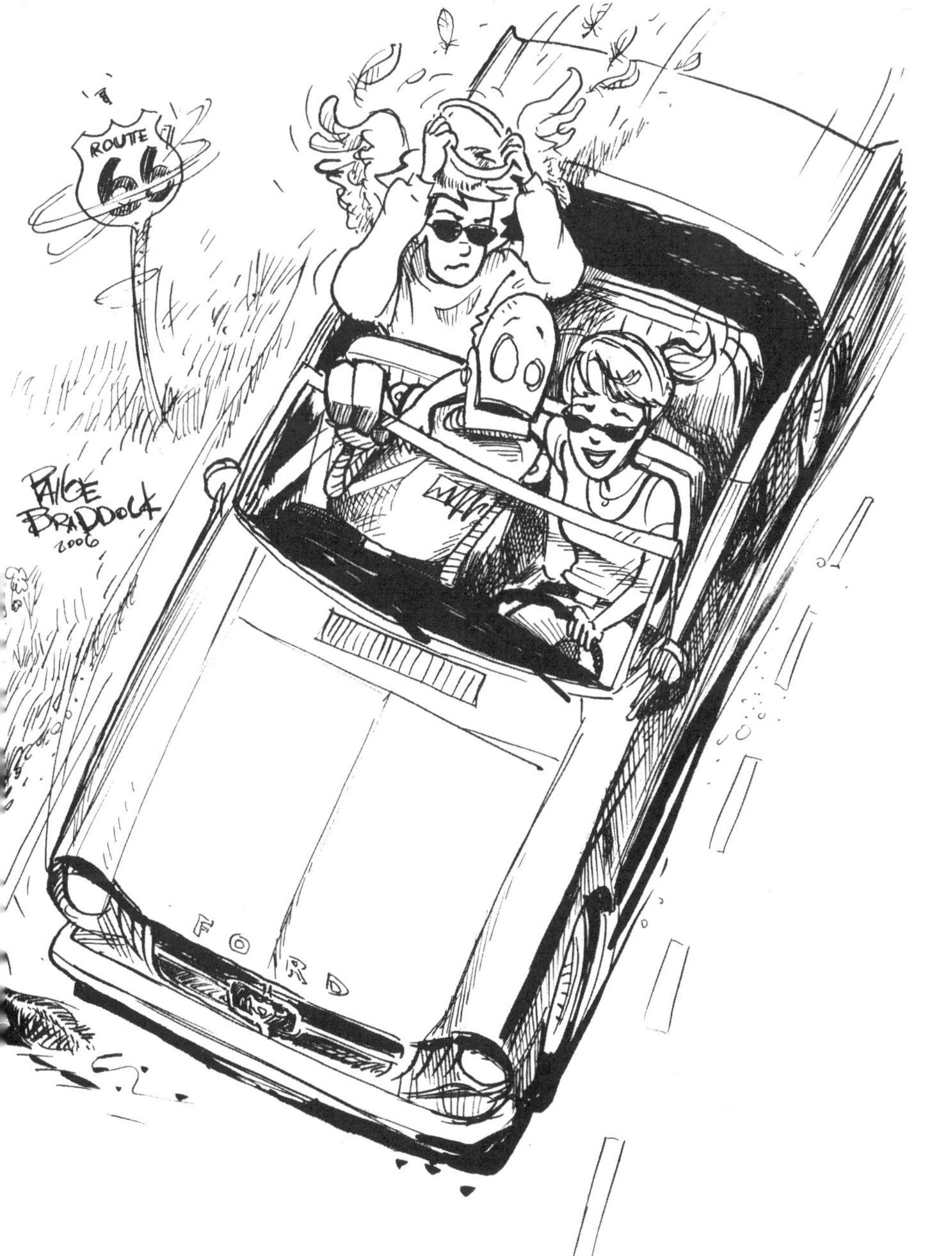
ROUTE
66
PAIGE
BRADDOCK
2006
FORD

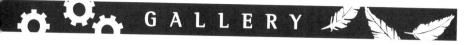

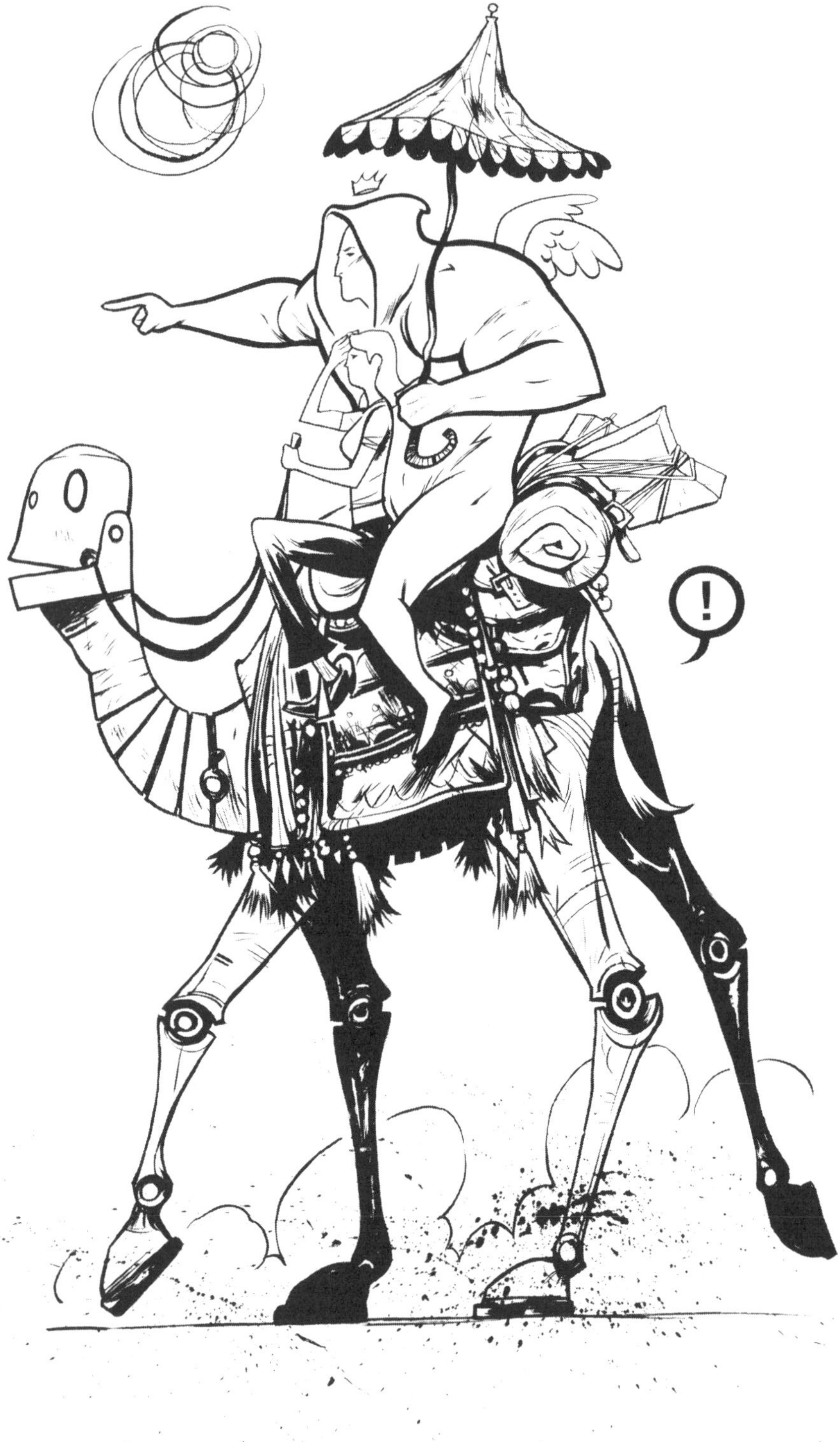
!

Continued from inside front cover...

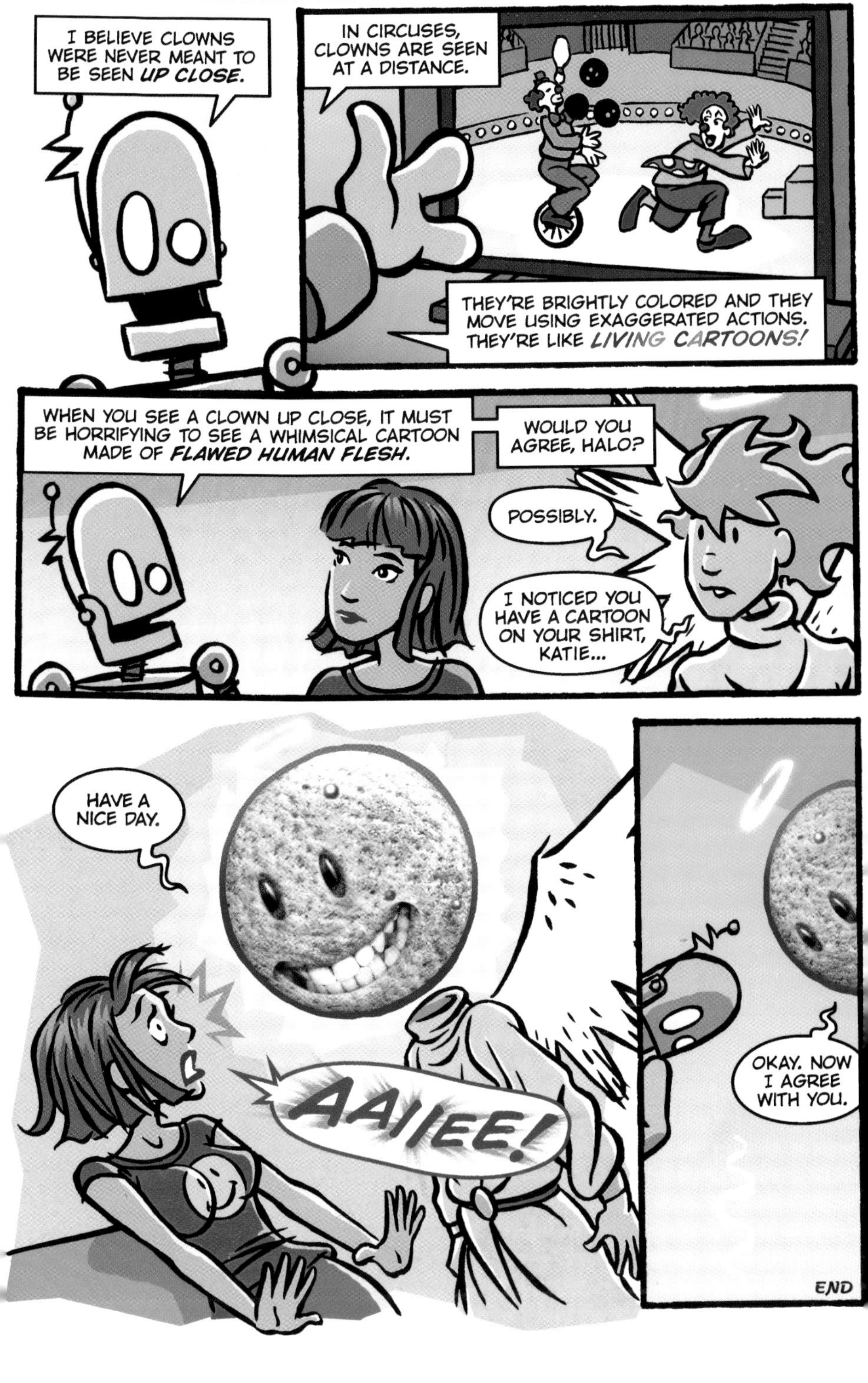
I BELIEVE CLOWNS WERE NEVER MEANT TO BE SEEN *UP CLOSE.*
IN CIRCUSES, CLOWNS ARE SEEN AT A DISTANCE.
THEY'RE BRIGHTLY COLORED AND THEY MOVE USING EXAGGERATED ACTIONS. THEY'RE LIKE *LIVING CARTOONS!*
WHEN YOU SEE A CLOWN UP CLOSE, IT MUST BE HORRIFYING TO SEE A WHIMSICAL CARTOON MADE OF *FLAWED HUMAN FLESH.*
WOULD YOU AGREE, HALO?
POSSIBLY.
I NOTICED YOU HAVE A CARTOON ON YOUR SHIRT, KATIE...
HAVE A NICE DAY.
AAIIEE!
OKAY. NOW I AGREE WITH YOU.
END

Welcome to the everyday adventures of an angel and a robot who live with a young, single woman. Logic, metaphysics, and human nature collide in this quirky, acclaimed series about the idiosyncrasies of life.

Find out why *Halo and Sprocket* is a favorite among critics, professionals, and fans alike...

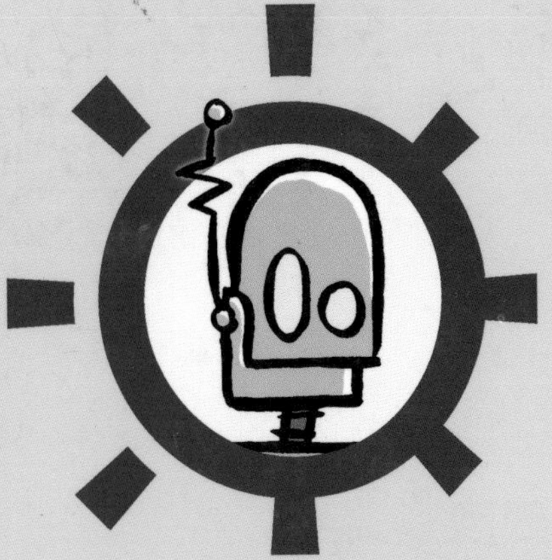

"It's the perfect sitcom that could only exist in comic book form, and thanks to Callen's sharp cartooning skills, quick wit and punchy delivery, it's about the funniest thing comic books have to offer."
– ***Randy Lander,*** **comic book critic, comicpants.com**

"Contrary to popular wisdom, there are a lot of good comics in the world and Halo & Sprocket is one of them, but no other comic can be as funny without being cruel, as sweet without being syrupy, as smart without being cynical, and even as romantic without being sentimental. Halo & Sprocket is a spring of undiluted originality– a commodity of which Callen seems to have an inexhaustible supply."
– ***Phil Hester,*** **comic book professional**

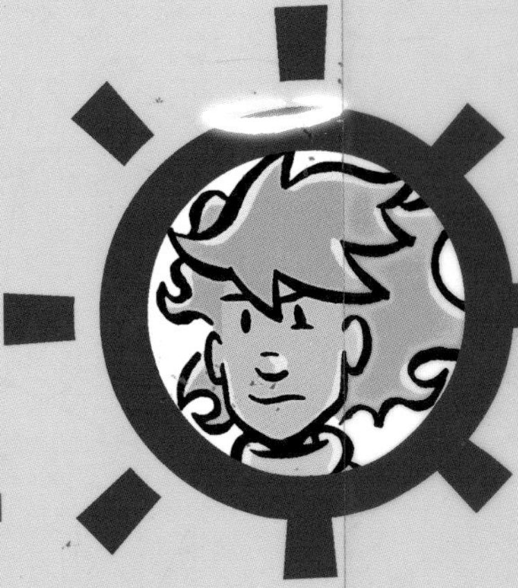

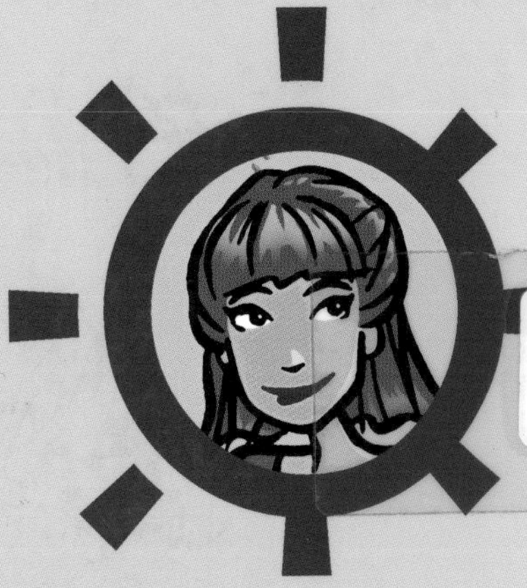

"I love Halo & Sprocket. It's not the same vapid crap."
– ***Jessie Hallum,*** **comic book fan**

$8.95

A division of SLG Publishing
9 781593 621315

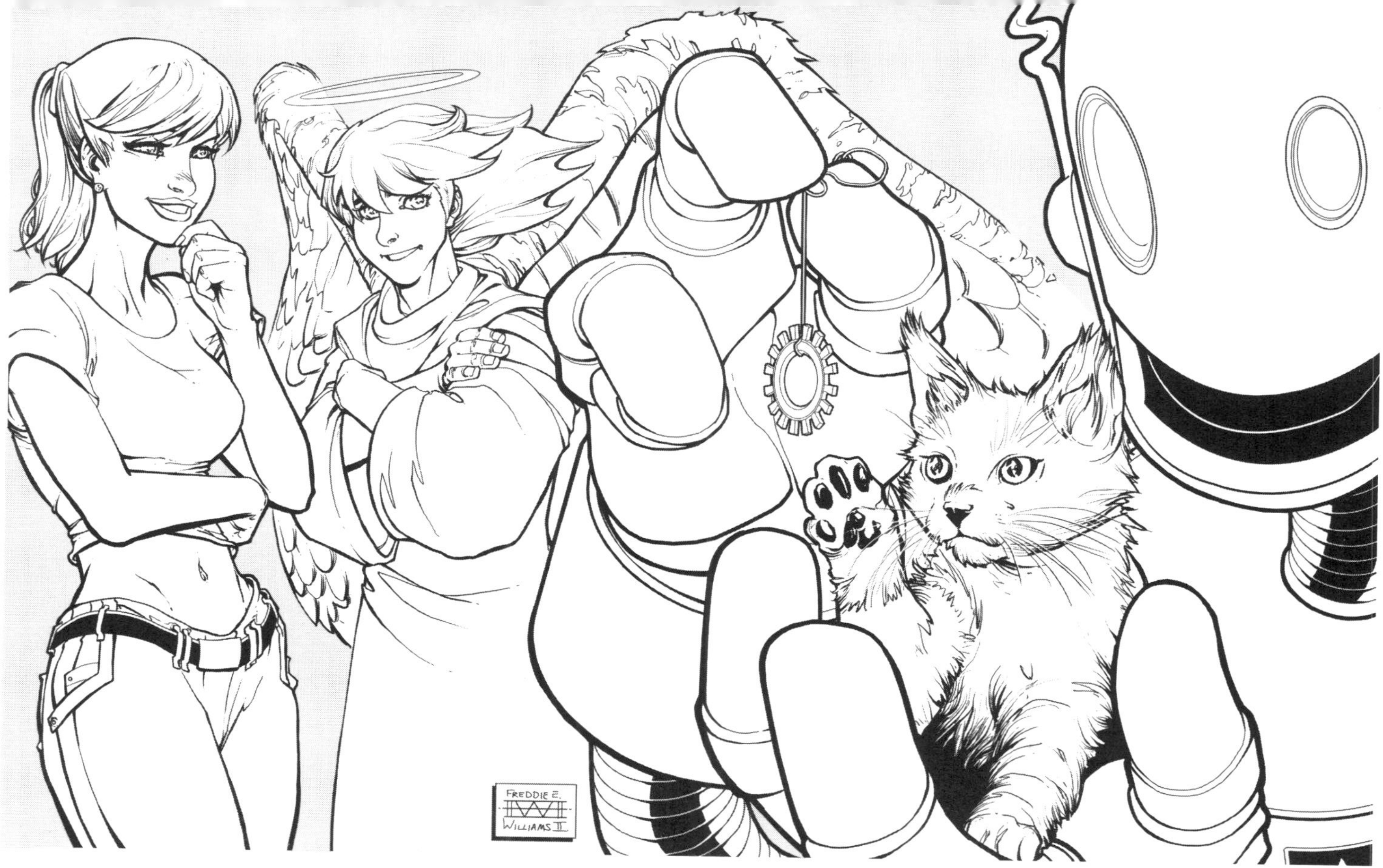
FREDDIE E. WILLIAMS II

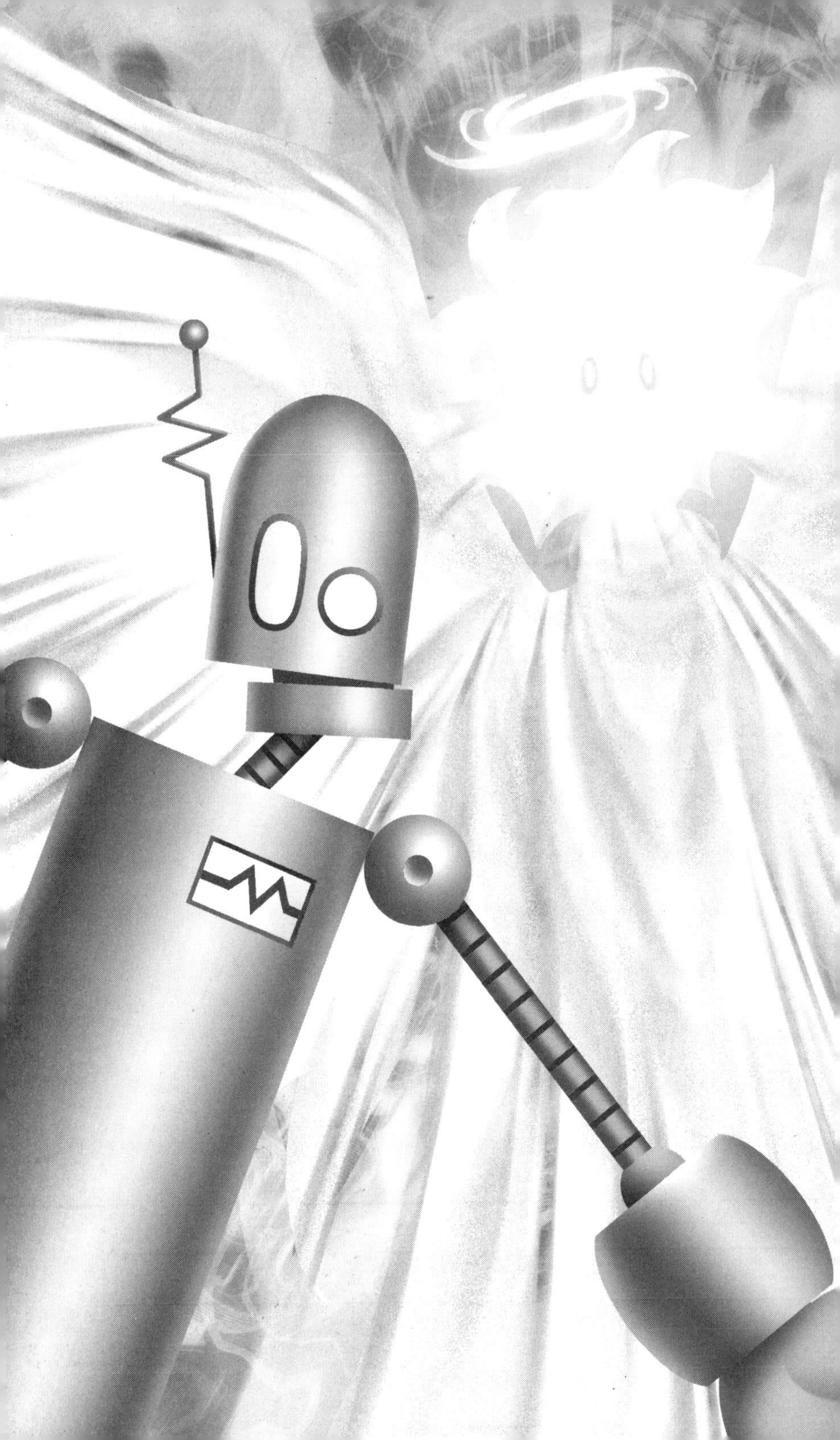